I COOK *in* COLOR

BRIGHT FLAVORS FROM MY KITCHEN

AND AROUND THE WORLD

I COOK in COLOR

BRIGHT FLAVORS FROM MY KITCHEN AND AROUND THE WORLD

Asha Gomez

and MARTHA HALL FOOSE

RUNNING PRESS

PHILADELPHIA

Running Press
Hachette Book Group
1290 Avenue of the Americas, New York, NY 10104
www.runningpress.com
@Running_Press

Printed in China
First Edition: October 2020

Published by Running Press, an imprint of Perseus Books, LLC, a
subsidiary of Hachette Book Group, Inc. The Running Press name and
logo is a trademark of the Hachette Book Group.

The Hachette Speakers Bureau provides a wide range of authors for speaking
events. To find out more, go to www.hachettespeakersbureau.com or call
(866) 376-6591.

The publisher is not responsible for websites (or their content) that are
not owned by the publisher.

Print book cover and interior design by Susan Van Horn.

Library of Congress Control Number: 2020936262

ISBNs: 978-0-7624-9558-0 (hardcover), 978-0-7624-9557-3 (ebook)

1010

10   9   8   7   6   5   4   3   2   1

To Bobby—
Thank you for being the very definition
of home: a foundation, a haven, and a light
in the window at the end of the day.
&
To Ethan—
You are my heart.
My whole heart.

CONTENTS

A World of Bright Flavors from My Kitchen

There's a big, colorful world out there, and I intend to share as much of it as I can with my lanky, long-haired teenage son, Ethan. I call this mission, "Walking the World with Ethan," hashtagging it and all. We might not make it to all our dream destinations, but that doesn't mean we won't sample their cuisine. Sometimes we just take a flavorful voyage from the comfort of our home kitchen.

Ethan and I live in the wildly cosmopolitan, categorically Southern city of Atlanta. It has been my home for 20 years. I came to these United States from India when I was a young teenager, and I've spent more of my life as an American than not. Yet some folks, at their first glance of me in an apron, make a hasty judgment that my kitchen must smell of curry all the time. Well, a couple of nights a week, they may be right, but on the whole, my kitchen smells of whatever inspires me. Those inspirations could be tastes that linger in my mind when I'm fresh from a trip abroad. They might come from a gleaming flash of color that caught my eye at one of this city's worldly farmers' markets. I find inspiration from the varied people we meet, and the colors they surround themselves in, like the bright-colored saris of the fisherwomen in Kerala; the embroidered skirts and scarves of the Peruvian women at the market, selling an astounding variety of potatoes, ranging from purple to orange; and the elderly women selling artichokes and wearing floral-embossed clogs at the outdoor market in Rome. Or Ethan might get curious about a country or region from his schoolwork, and soon we are both gung-ho to see what they favor on the plate. I guess what I'm saying is this: I cook a lot like the folks I surround myself with—an eclectic mix.

There is no mistaking the power of color to draw us in. When my son was young, like most kids, he started with the basic kindergarten pack of fat crayons, featuring Roy G. Biv's rainbow of colors. But as Ethan has grown and we talk about the world and explore the myriad of colors that can be mixed and mingled, we now go for the deluxe Crayola box with a sharpener on the back, giving us a much broader palette from which to draw.

My childhood in Kerala was awash in brilliant colors, like the ombre shades of blue out across the Arabian Sea, the vermillion and mahogany shades of ground chilies, and verdant tea estates in the mountains rolling in green and umber. All are parts of my technicolored nostalgia. In my mind's eye my mother's kitchen always has a slight turmeric-gold cast. The sight of sugar baby watermelons, with their vibrant pink hearts exposed, immediately takes me to a long, sultry Georgia summer. The color of fresh white cream propels me into visions of fluffy desserts. What the eyes make welcome to the heart inspires me to swing my pantry doors wide open and engage my soul in my cooking.

Sights inspire me, but aren't my only guiding forces. If I were blindfolded, my sense of smell would lead me like a thieving cartoon character drawn to a pie cooling on a windowsill. My sense of taste might make me shudder, make my shoulders rise, and make my lips pucker when I bite down on bitter melon. We are all guided by a world of influences that sway our tastes from one day to the next. Interests are sometimes fleeting or long-held.

And for our health's sake, we eat a wide variety of brightly colored foods, because it's one of the best and easiest ways to make sure we get the nutrition we need. So, my advice is this: Trust your eyes. If a food has an attractive color, chances are it's beneficial for you. Many of the colorful herbs and spices used throughout this book have health-giving properties, too. Reading the spice primer from my first book, *My Two Souths: Blending the Flavors of India into a Southern Kitchen*, might come in handy when purchasing many of the ingredients used in these pages. Some elements called for in these recipes might not be familiar to some folks. Well, we live in a wondrous time where almost any ingredient imaginable can be found online and arrive on your doorstep in a day or two. I've offered substitutions for many ingredients, but encourage you to search out components that will lend authentic flavor to these dishes.

All in all, *I Cook in Color* is about "cognizant cooking," being aware of, and welcoming the vivid, color-filled world into your kitchen. Conversing around countertops, making friends at the market, dreaming around dessert, and exploring all the bounty that surrounds us—these are the elements that can make your world not just colorful but wildly flavorful as well.

—*Asha Gomez*

CHAPTER ONE:

colorful drinks
to sip *and* savor

Virgin Fresh Tomato Watermelon Mary

I love fresh tomato juice. It's my summer jam! There is a famous salad made with watermelon and tomato that pops up on the recipe sites every summer. I thought, "This would make for a delightful cocktail." So here's my take on a Bloody Mary with a hint of sweetness from watermelon—perfect for those lazy summer afternoons.

MAKES **2 SERVINGS**

For the Cocktail

6 large fresh plum tomatoes, peeled

1 cup watermelon, cut into small cubes

2 cups water

2 garlic cloves

1 tablespoon Worcestershire sauce

1 tablespoon Pete's hot sauce or your favorite brand

1 serrano chili, seeded

¼ teaspoon kosher salt

2 tablespoons granulated sugar

For Garnish

4 cornichons

2 small, thin watermelon wedges

2 tender celery stalks with leaves

Blend all the cocktail ingredients in a blender. Pour into two tall glasses.

Garnish each one with cornichons, a watermelon wedge, and a celery stalk.

NOTES

Use whatever variety of ripe tomato catches your eye at the market.

Serve these "cocktails" with little cubes of feta cheese for snacking.

Morning Sunshine

Every time I gain a few pounds, I resort to juicing to get back to my fighting weight. It seems to work well for me. I also just love juicing at least one meal a day when I can, usually breakfast. This carrot, cantaloupe, fresh turmeric juice is one of my all-time favorites. I can just about put it together while I'm still half asleep.

MAKES **2 SERVINGS**

4 large carrots

4 cups cubed cantaloupe

1-inch piece fresh turmeric

Put all the ingredients through a juicer and serve.

NOTES

You definitely need a juicer to make this drink.

If you can't find fresh turmeric, mix a teaspoon of turmeric powder into your juice.

All-Day Herb Water

I drink a lot of water throughout the day, but, let's face it, after a while, plain water can get pretty dull. One of my first tasks of the day is to prepare my jug of herb-infused water by clipping some of this and that from my windowsill garden. The herb flavor intensifies as it sits throughout the day. As my strength wanes, the water gains potency, helping me keep up the pace of a busy day.

MAKES 1 GALLON

1 gallon room-temperature water

3 stems lavender (with or without flowers)

3 sprigs rosemary

6 sprigs thyme

6 sprigs mint

½ English cucumber, chopped

Combine all ingredients is a large jug. Refrigerate for more extended storage or if you prefer cold water. I take mine straight up.

Rosemary Lemonade

My home is a bustling place. Most weekends, if I'm not working or travel-ing, I have guests over for cocktails on a Saturday night or an early Sunday supper. My guest list is ever-evolving, but my dear friend George and his teenage kids have a standing invitation. My son, Ethan, loves this time with friends. This lemonade, saturated with rosemary, is a little stylish, which the teenagers seem to enjoy. It also takes well to a shot of vodka, something the grown folks appreciate.

MAKES 6 SERVINGS

7 cups water, divided

1 cup granulated white sugar

6 sprigs fresh rosemary, plus more for garnish

2/3 cup freshly squeezed lemon juice

6 cups crushed ice

Make a simple syrup by boiling 1 cup of water with 1 cup of sugar and the rosemary for 5 minutes. Remove from the heat and pour into a large pitcher. Let it cool before chilling in the refrigerator.

Once the syrup has chilled, add the lemon juice and the remaining water. Serve over the crushed ice and garnish with rosemary sprigs.

NOTES

You can make so many different flavors of simple syrup. One of my favorites, which I always have on hand, is cardamom simple syrup. Use about 10 pods of crushed whole green cardamom pods, instead of the rosemary, and follow this recipe.

Emerald Potion

I've never been a big fan of most green juice concoctions because most don't taste, well, all that tasty. But here's my version of a green juice with plenty of fruit to sweeten it up. I don't know if it will detox you, but I do know I always feel better after having a glass!

MAKES **2 SERVINGS**

1 cup peeled, roughly chopped Granny Smith apples

2 cups chopped cantaloupe

2 bananas, peeled and sliced

2 cups baby spinach

Juice of 1 lime

2 cups cold coconut water

Put all the ingredients in a blender and blend until smooth. Pour and drink.

NOTE

Sometimes, I add a few dates to this revitalizing, blended beverage.

Golden Haldi Dood:
Turmeric Milk with Honey

A few years back, on one of my trips to New York City, while walking the streets, I came across a sweet little tea shop. And since I am a tea lover, I decided to take a moment to have a cup of tea. Scrolling through the menu, I came across Warm Turmeric Milk, priced at $9 a cup. Sticker shock at first, but I just had to indulge. One sip, and it took me back to my childhood. When we were growing up, *Haldi Dood* was a staple elixir for a sore throat. The warm, sweet milk and turmeric were a welcome panacea when we weren't feeling well. Somehow over the years, I had forgotten about this golden milk, but after that pricy reminder, it is now a warming delight at home, even when I'm not under the weather.

MAKES 2 SERVINGS

2 cups whole milk

1 teaspoon turmeric powder, plus more if desired

1 teaspoon cardamom powder

2 tablespoons raw honey

In a small pot over medium to low heat, whisk together all the ingredients. Heat for 5 minutes, whisking often until the milk is warmed. Be careful not to let the milk boil over.

NOTES

You've probably already heard of the health benefits of turmeric, as the spice is becoming tremendously popular in the States. It is hailed as one of the most therapeutic spices in the world, with its antibacterial properties.

My mother used it much the same way as many mothers use Neosporin, swabbing powdered turmeric into all our scrapes and scratches and then bandaging us up. Trust me when I say it works!

Mango Yogurt Madness

The sight or smell of mangoes sweeps me up into a nostalgic dreamland. One of my fondest memories from my teenage years in India is making midnight runs to the lassi shop down the street during summertime. It was our neighborhood equivalent of an ice cream parlor serving up shakes made with tangy yogurt.

I don't always have access to the best fresh mangoes here in the United States. But the one thing that is readily available all year round is mango pulp in cans from India. The Alphonso or Kesar mango works best for this shake.

NOTES

The serving size on these is 8-ounce portions. It's a creamy shake, and I think that is just the perfect size.

MAKES 4 SERVINGS

2 cups prepared mango pulp, or fresh or frozen diced mango

2 cups plain yogurt

2 teaspoons cardamom powder

2 tablespoons granulated sugar

In a blender, mix all the ingredients together for a minute or two until smooth. Chill in the refrigerator for a half-hour or serve over ice.

Fig and Cashew Milk Shake

Somehow when I think of fruit shakes and smoothies, I always associate them with summer. However, this is a perfect shake for fall and winter months when the markets aren't exactly overflowing with fresh fruits. It's simple, it's delicious, and, frankly, it's a meal in itself. This fig and cashew milk shake is a perfect breakfast on the go, filled with fiber and protein. It also contains vitamins A, B_1, B_2, and D, and potassium, magnesium, copper, iron, and phosphorus.

MAKES 2 SERVINGS

1 cup Kalamata crown (*goumas*) dried figs, about 12, roughly chopped

2 cups water

½ cup raw cashews

2 cups cold whole milk, divided

½ cup raw honey

Soak the dried figs in 2 cups of water overnight or for at least an hour, or until they are rehydrated. Remove the figs from the water and discard the water. In a blender, combine the figs and cashews with 1 cup of the milk, and blend to make a smooth puree. Add the remainder of the milk, along with the honey, and blend to the consistency of a smoothie. Drink immediately.

NOTES

I have found the best quality dried figs at Persian markets. Soaking the dried fruit is very important; if you skip this step, the texture of the shake is not as smooth.

Ruby Red Beet Juice: The "Mommy Boost"

This juice gives me life every morning! I've been a regular morning juicer for about a year and a half, and have never felt more energized. Beets are a great source of vitamin B_6, folate, manganese, and iron. I like to start with all the ingredients chilled, so this invigorating blend is refreshing right out of the juicer.

MAKES **2 SERVINGS**

2 medium beets, cut into 2-inch pieces

1 inch fresh turmeric

1 inch fresh ginger

2 green apples, cut into 2-inch pieces

2 carrots, cut into 2-inch pieces

Juice the beets, then the turmeric and ginger. Follow by juicing the apples and carrots. Stir well and serve.

NOTE

This juice can also be made in a blender by adding 1 cup of water, blending, then straining the juice through a fine-mesh sieve.

Dreamy Spiced
Hot Chocolate

In my kitchen, the only way to make hot chocolate is to use unsweetened cocoa powder and condensed milk, along with a trio of spices. An intricately carved wooden whisk, called a *molinillo* in Latin America and a *btirol* in the Philippines, is a tool designed specifically for frothing hot chocolate and a perfect gift for culinarily inclined friends. You use it by rubbing the handle back and forth between your palms. It's a fun little ritual. You could also use a small whisk to whip up this richly spiced, dreamy chocolate warmer, but it is not quite as exciting.

MAKES 2 SERVINGS

2 cups whole milk

2 cups water

½ cup sweetened condensed milk

2 star anise

1 teaspoon ancho chili powder

1 teaspoon cardamom powder

4 tablespoons unsweetened, dark, Dutch-process cocoa powder

In a 2-quart pot on low heat, pour the milk, water, and condensed milk, and mix well. Add the star anise, chili powder, and cardamom, and let the liquid simmer on a low heat for 15 minutes to infuse all the spices into the milk mixture. Add the cocoa powder and mix well, using a small whisk or *molinillo* to create a nice froth on top. Pour into cups and serve piping hot.

NOTES
Feel free to add more condensed milk if it's not sweet enough for your palate. The condensed milk makes this hot chocolate really velvety.

Assam Tea Time

Tea gardens in Assam do not follow Indian Standard Time (IST), which is observed throughout India and Sri Lanka. The local time in Assam's tea gardens, known as "Tea Garden Time" or Bagantime, is an hour ahead of the standard time. The system was put in place by the British, and the reasoning behind it was that the early sunrise in the far eastern part of the country necessitated an hour jump in the region to get to work at an earlier hour on the clock.

In my culinary event venue, Third Space, I started making this tea for my guests who were lactose intolerant and couldn't enjoy my chai. Now I sometimes serve this clove tea instead of chai, which usually accompanies dessert at our dinners. It's an excellent way to end a meal.

MAKES 4 SERVINGS

4 cups water

4 tablespoons black Assam tea

4 cloves, coarsely crushed

4 teaspoons powdered or shaved palm sugar or light brown sugar

Bring the water to a boil in a kettle. Pour the water into a teapot. (I use a teapot with a built-in strainer.) Add the tea and cloves and let the tea steep for 3 minutes. Strain and pour into cups. Sweeten each cup with a teaspoon of palm sugar. Drink hot.

Pretty in Pink
Rose Milk

As a kid growing up in India, there was no chocolate milk or strawberry milk, but there was always rose milk. And, boy, did I love it. One way my mother could get me to drink milk was by adding sweet *rooh afza*. The bright red syrup, flavored with rose essence and other botanicals, turns milk a lovely, princessy, shade of pink, which I found especially appealing when I was little. My mother also added *sabja*, which are sweet basil seeds, to boost the nutritional aspects of this blushing beverage. The tiny black seeds add a good bit of calcium, magnesium, and iron.

Rooh afza means "refresher of the soul" and this drink is truly a delight.

NOTE

You can find rooh afza *and basil seeds at most Indian or South Asian grocery stores, or you can buy both online.*

MAKES 4 SERVINGS

4 cups chilled whole milk

6 tablespoons *rooh afza* syrup

4 teaspoons basil seeds, soaked in ¼ cup water for a few minutes until plump

Pour the milk into a glass pitcher and mix in the *rooh afza* syrup. Add the basil seeds and serve over ice or chill in the refrigerator until you're ready to serve it.

CHAPTER TWO:

bright salads

Thai Green Papaya Salad

I've always loved papaya salad; it's my go-to, always dependable starter whenever I dine in Thai restaurants. So, learning how to make a proper Thai salad at home was high on my "Learn this, Asha" list. I'm usually able to decipher flavors and figure out ingredients when I try a new dish, and I knew fish sauce and lime were a couple of the main ingredients. Then I met Faye Poone, a fellow chef who is from Thailand, and asked her to come over and let me cook dinner for her one evening. She quickly offered to cook for me instead and taught me how to make this papaya salad, which became a staple in my kitchen.

This is a salad you can dress a little ahead of time. The papaya soaks up the dressing, wonderfully melding the tart, sweet, fresh flavors. I prefer to make the dressing with a mortar and pestle, but it can be whipped up in a food processor, too. You may want to invest in a julienne peeler, especially if you plan to make this salad as often as I do.

1 bunch cilantro, well washed (look for bunches with the roots still attached)

2 tablespoons small dried shrimp

2 tablespoons fish sauce

6 tablespoons fresh lime juice

4 tablespoons grated palm sugar or dark brown sugar

4 garlic cloves

2 Thai red chilies

1 carrot, peeled and thinly sliced into strips

12 cherry tomatoes, halved

¼ pound haricot verts or tender green beans, trimmed

1 medium green papaya, peeled, halved, seeded, and thinly sliced

Separate the leaves from the stems of the cilantro. Using a large mortar and pestle or a food processor, grind the dried shrimp, fish sauce, lime juice, palm sugar, cilantro stems and roots, garlic, and Thai chilies into a thick paste for the dressing.

In a large bowl, toss together the carrots, tomatoes, beans, papaya, and cilantro leaves. Toss the salad with the dressing and serve.

NOTE

Tiny, salty, dried shrimp are used around the globe in cuisines as varied as African, Mexican, Brazilian, and Asian. They impart a flavor that is hard to pinpoint, but missed if absent. Look for them in small bags in international markets of all sorts.

Bombay Boiled Peanut Salad with Black Salt

If you are an adventurous and imaginative boiled peanut lover, this salad will whisk you away to the fantastic food stalls on the humming streets of India. Figuring out the easiest way to make this peanut salad without having to spend half a day boiling whole raw peanuts and shucking them is another story. My dear and gifted friend Chef Vish Bhatt told me that I could just boil raw shelled peanuts. What a time—and cleanup saver!

I usually extol the virtues of perfectly ripe mangoes, but in this recipe, I am calling for a semi-ripened mango. The mango needs to be firm and slightly sweet and sour for this salad to come together just right.

MAKES 4 SERVINGS

2 cups shelled, boiled peanuts

1 tablespoon kosher salt

1 small semi-ripe firm mango, peeled and finely chopped

1 small red onion, finely chopped

1 plum tomato, seeded and finely chopped

1 jalapeño pepper, seeded and finely chopped

½ cup cilantro leaves, finely chopped

½ teaspoon black salt

Juice of 1 lime

Toss all of the ingredients in a medium-size bowl. Serve at room temperature.

NOTES

If you'd like more heat in this salad, leave the seeds in the jalapeño. And if it's not mango season and you can't get your hands on a mango, use a Granny Smith apple instead.

Caramelized Fig Salad with Radicchio and Hazelnuts

For me, fig season is a happy season. Black mission figs may be my favorite type, but I also adore brown turkey figs, which are more commonly found here in the South. I can't walk past these beauties if I see them at a market—they will most certainly be coming home with me! I love them in salads, as a preserve, or fresh drizzled with raw honey and sprinkled with freshly crushed pepper. I also love them caramelized, which is what I do for this salad. The combination of sweet figs, bitter roasted radicchio, tangy feta, and sweet honey touches every flavor note on your palate.

MAKES 4 SERVINGS

4 tablespoons extra-virgin olive oil, divided

1 pound fresh black mission figs, halved

4 small heads of radicchio quartered lengthwise, keeping the core intact

¼ pound crumbled feta

½ cup raw honey

¼ cup toasted hazelnuts, whole

2 teaspoons coarsely ground black pepper

1 teaspoon pink Himalayan salt

In a medium skillet, heat 2 tablespoons of olive oil over high heat. Add the figs, flesh side down, and let the figs caramelize for about a minute or two until they're golden brown. Turn them over and cook them for another minute, then remove the figs from the pan, and set them aside. Add the remaining 2 tablespoons of oil to the pan and add the quartered radicchio, cut side down, and sear until golden brown. This should take no more than a minute. Remove from the pan and set aside.

Assemble the salad on a large platter. Lay the figs and radicchio on the plate and sprinkle with the crumbled feta. Drizzle the raw honey evenly over the salad. Sprinkle with the toasted hazelnuts, pepper, and salt.

NOTES

Figs are in season two times a year—in the summertime around June and again in the fall from late August to early October. The varieties readily available in the United States are black mission figs, brown turkey figs, tiger figs, and champagne figs. You can't go wrong using any of them!

Nice Salmon Salad

I love to spend a day with my "Sister Fires" (the term of endearment I have bestowed on my spirited group of girlfriends). So I don't want to spend too much time holed up in the kitchen when I have them over. This composed salad is a deliciously simple centerpiece for a casual luncheon with them. Everything is prepared before they arrive so I can meet them at the door with a relaxed smile.

This salad is inspired by the salads served along coastal France. I give it a little "Asha treatment" by drizzling the salmon with some olive oil, tempered with mustard seeds.

For the Salmon

1 (4-pound) slab of wild salmon

½ cup olive oil

2 teaspoons kosher salt

2 teaspoons sweet paprika

For the Green Beans

½ teaspoon baking soda

½ pound green beans

For the Eggs

6 seven-minute eggs, cut in halves

For the Dressing

½ cup mayonnaise

¼ cup extra-virgin olive oil

¼ cup honey

¼ cup spicy, grainy mustard

¼ cup lemon juice

1 teaspoon kosher salt

For the Tempered Oil

2 tablespoons olive oil

2 teaspoons black mustard seeds

For the Salad

1 cup Niçoise olives or Kalamata olives, pitted

3 cups frisee

3 cups Bibb lettuce leaves

1½ pounds heirloom tomatoes, quartered

10 caper berries

To make the salmon: Heat the oven to 425°F. Line a sheet pan with parchment paper, place the salmon skin-side down on the pan. Drizzle the salmon with ½ cup of the olive oil. Sprinkle the salt and paprika evenly all over the salmon and roast in the oven for 10 to 12 minutes. Remove from the oven and set aside.

To make the green beans: Bring a large pot of water to a boil, add a pinch of baking soda, and then drop in the green beans. Blanch for 3 minutes, remove the beans with a slotted spoon, and place the beans in an ice bath or cool under running cold water.

To make the eggs: Bring a pot of water to a boil, place your eggs in boiling water for 7 minutes.

Remove the eggs from the water and place them in an ice bath or under cold running water. Peel the eggs and set aside. Slice the eggs in half.

To make the dressing: In a bowl, whisk all the ingredients together and set aside.

To make the tempered oil: Heat a small skillet over medium to high. Heat 2 tablespoons of olive oil and add the mustard seeds. When the mustard seeds pop, remove the pan from the heat.

To assemble the salad: Place the salmon in the center of the platter and pour half the dressing over the fish. Pour the tempered oil over the salmon. Arrange all the remaining ingredients around the fish. Serve with the remaining dressing on the side.

NOTES

Niçoise olives are a French favorite, produced in the region around the French Riviera. Brine-cured, they come in colors that range from deep, almost black-purple to pale green to light taupe. These petite olives have an intensely savory flavor and often come packed with herbs.

Jade Salad

If you have been in a tossed salad rut, change things up with this marvelous mixture of butter lettuce, curly frisee, and sunflower sprouts tossed with green raisins, avocado, and creamy blue cheese, finished with a drizzle of honey.

MAKES 4 SERVINGS

2 garlic cloves

Zest and juice of 2 limes

1 cup mint leaves

1 cup cilantro leaves

2 tablespoons mayonnaise
(I prefer Duke's)

1 teaspoon kosher salt

½ cup extra-virgin olive oil

1 large head of butter lettuce

2 cups frisee

2 cups sunflower sprouts

2 large avocados, diced

1 cup crumbled blue cheese

¼ cup green raisins

2 tablespoons honey

In a food processor, combine the garlic, lime zest and juice, mint leaves, cilantro leaves, mayonnaise, salt, and olive oil. Pulse to combine. Set the dressing aside.

Place the butter lettuce, frisee, sunflower sprouts, and avocado in a large bowl. Pour the dressing in and lightly toss. Add crumbled blue cheese, raisins, and drizzle with honey. Serve immediately.

NOTE
Green raisins are often used in Persian cooking. Golden or sultana raisins can be substituted in this recipe.

Crying Tiger Grilled Beef Salad

Thai food has become a popular cuisine for the American palate, and I believe it has some of the easiest, most accessible recipes for home cooks. If you've never experimented with Thai cooking, then go buy some fish sauce and liquid palm syrup, and you'll be able to cook up all kinds of Thai dishes. Another plus is that the use of oil in Thai cooking is rather minimal, so it can actually be a rather healthy, delicious, and uncomplicated option on weeknights at home. This salad certainly is.

MAKES 4 SERVINGS

For the Steak

2 pounds sirloin steak

1 teaspoon kosher salt

2 teaspoons coarsely ground black pepper

1 bunch fresh romaine lettuce

1 bunch fresh Thai basil stems and leaves

For the Dipping Sauce

2 tablespoons fish sauce

½ cup freshly squeezed lime juice

2 tablespoons palm syrup or raw sugar

1 teaspoon ground toasted rice (see Notes)

2 Thai chilies, finely chopped

1 scallion thinly sliced

½ cup cilantro finely chopped

To make the steak: Pat the steak dry. Season the steak all over with salt and pepper. Heat a grill pan over high heat. Sear the steak on all sides then reduce the heat to medium and cook to medium-rare (130°F–135°F). Remove the steak from the grill pan and let the steak rest for 10 minutes before slicing the steak at an angle against the grain into thin strips. While the steak is resting, prepare the dipping sauce.

To make the dipping sauce: Mix all the ingredients well, and set aside as a dipping sauce to serve with the beef salad.

To assemble: Serve the steak alongside romaine, Thai basil, and dipping sauce.

NOTES

My favorite brand of fish sauce is Squid Brand Fish Sauce.

If you can't find ground toasted rice, roast 2 tablespoons of raw jasmine rice in a pan over medium heat until it is brown as a paper grocery sack. Then use a coffee or spice grinder to grind the rice to about the texture of espresso.

CHAPTER THREE:

luscious soups *and* comforting stews

Clove-Infused Tomato Soup with Puffy Lids

This soup is an ode to one of my favorite restaurants in Atlanta, a quaint, neighborhood French bistro called Bread & Butterfly. That place is my home away from home, be it for a solitary breakfast in the mornings, lunch meetings with dear friends, or dinner with my boy. Their one dish that stands out for me is the tomato soup that Chef Billy Allin created. It's perfect, especially on fall evenings. It's a little time-consuming because there are a few steps to preparing it. You will cook it on the stovetop, puree it, and then bake it in the oven cloaked in a layer of puff pastry. I can assure you, however, that it is totally worth the effort. This soup will really wow your guests at a dinner party.

Rainbow Chard and Kabocha Pumpkin Bean Soup

Fall just may be my favorite time of year. After the hot summer months, I look forward to the cool weather and the magic of soup season. This white cannellini bean and rainbow chard soup is filling and full of flavor. Celebrate fall with this soup, bobbing with pumpkin!

MAKES 6 TO 8 SERVINGS

¼ cup olive oil

1 large yellow onion, diced

2 celery stalks, thinly sliced

6 garlic cloves, finely chopped

1 tablespoon fresh thyme leaves

6 whole green cardamom pods, crushed

2 teaspoons white pepper

1 tablespoon kosher salt

1 (14½-ounce) can whole, peeled tomatoes

4 cups vegetable broth

2 (15-ounce) cans cannellini beans, drained

1 cup Kabocha pumpkin, cut into ½-inch pieces

4 cups chopped rainbow Swiss chard

Heat the olive oil in a large Dutch oven over medium heat. Add the onions and cook, stirring occasionally, for 3 minutes or until the onions are translucent. Add the celery and garlic, and stir for another 2 minutes.

Add the thyme, cardamom, and white pepper, and salt, and mix well. Add the tomatoes and cook for 5 minutes until the tomatoes break down; add the broth and bring it to a boil. Lower the heat, add the beans and pumpkin, mix well, and cook for 20 minutes or until tender. Remove from the heat. Add the rainbow chard and mix well. Serve immediately.

NOTES

Don't overcook the beans and let them get mushy. Also, turn off the heat as soon as you put in the rainbow chard, the residual heat will wilt the greens, and the stems will still have a crunch to them.

Yellow Split Pea Sambar with Turnips, Eggplant, and Butternut Squash

My mother's influence inevitably finds its way into everything I do. She's the foundation of so much I learned in life and in the kitchen. My love of spice definitely comes from her. In Kerala, *sambar* is a classic southern Indian stew eaten at just about every meal. For breakfast, we eat it with steamed rice cakes, called *idli*, or rice crepes, called *dosa*. For lunch and dinner, we eat it with steamed rice and fish curry or braised beef dishes. I love eating sambar over steamed rice, or I just eat a big bowl of the *sambar*; it's a meal in itself.

You need to follow a few steps I think of as "phases" in concocting this dish. But don't let that put you off. Take your time, and it will work out deliciously!

For the First Phase

1 tablespoon ghee or unsalted clarified butter

1 teaspoon cumin seeds

1 teaspoon turmeric powder

1 large onion, chopped

2 garlic cloves, smashed

½ cup yellow split peas (*toovar dal*)

3 cups water

2 teaspoons kosher salt

For the Second Phase

1 tablespoon ghee or clarified unsalted butter

2 large Roma tomatoes, quartered

1 cup diced Yukon gold potatoes

1 cup diced turnips

1 cup diced Japanese eggplants

12 okra pods, split down the center

1 tablespoon sambar powder

1 teaspoon tamarind paste

1 cup water

1 teaspoon kosher salt

For the Third Phase

1 tablespoon ghee or clarified unsalted butter

1 teaspoon brown mustard seeds

6 dried whole red chilies

½ cup chopped cilantro

To make the first phase: Heat a large Dutch oven over medium heat. Place in the Dutch oven the ghee and cumin seeds. Let the cumin seeds get toasted; this takes about 1 minute. Add the turmeric to the pot, along with the onions. Cook and stir the onions for about 3 minutes or until translucent. Add the garlic and cook, stirring for another minute. Add the split peas, water, and salt, and stir well. Let the liquid come to a boil. Cover and reduce the heat to medium-low. Cook with the lid on for 20 to 25 minutes, or until the split peas are cooked through and soft but still hold their shape.

To make the second phase: While the split peas are cooking, heat a large skillet over medium-high heat and add the ghee to the pan. Add the vegetables and sambar powder. Stir in the tamarind paste, and mix well. Add the water and salt. Let the vegetables cook until all the liquid has evaporated (they don't have to be cooked through). Transfer the vegetables into the Dutch oven with the cooked yellow peas and cook for another 15 minutes or until the vegetables are cooked through. Remove from the heat.

To make the third phase: Heat a small skillet over medium-high heat. Add the ghee, mustard seeds, and the dry red chilies, and let the mustard seeds pop; this should take less than a minute. Remove from the heat and pour the hot ghee mixture into the sambar. Add the cilantro and serve.

NOTES

The most crucial ingredient for this dish is the sambar powder. It is a mixture that includes coriander seed, fenugreek seeds, cumin seed, black peppercorns, red chilies, and asafetida. If you can't find yellow split peas, try using red lentils in their place.

Fish Head Stew

I grew up eating whole fish in my mother's kitchen. As in every other kitchen in Kerala, there was rarely such thing as filleting fish and deboning it. You cooked the entire fish, unless it was really huge, and then it was cut into bone-in steaks. Even when we moved to the United States, my mother rarely cooked boneless fillets. This dish is on rotation in my kitchen at least two to three times a month. My son, Ethan, craves it just as much as I do.

MAKES 4 SERVINGS

2 (1-pound) whole black bass, cleaned, head and tail intact, and cut into 3 pieces widthwise (head, center, and tail)

2 teaspoons kosher salt, divided

4 medium-size Roma tomatoes, quartered

1 small red onion, quartered

2 garlic cloves

2 teaspoons turmeric powder

2 teaspoons chili powder

2 teaspoons hot paprika

2 teaspoons tamarind paste

2 cups water

1 teaspoon dark brown sugar

2 tablespoons vegetable oil

2 teaspoons black mustard seeds

2 small shallots, skin on and quartered

10 curry leaves

1 tablespoon finely chopped ginger

2 cups steamed jasmine rice, for serving

Season the fish with a teaspoon of salt and set aside. In a blender, combine the tomatoes, onions, garlic, turmeric, chili powder, paprika, tamarind paste, water, 1 teaspoon of salt, and the brown sugar. Blend to a liquid consistency. Pour the liquid from the blender into a shallow pot and turn the heat to medium-high. Let the liquid cook for 5 minutes. Add the fish to the pot and cover with a lid; lower the heat to medium-low and cook for 5 minutes. Remove the lid and cook for another 5 minutes. In the meantime, place the oil in a small skillet over medium heat. Add the mustard seeds; when the mustard seeds pop, add the shallots and let the shallots get golden brown, about 5 minutes. Add the curry leaves and remove the pan from the heat. Splash this tempered oil over the stew and serve warm with some steamed jasmine rice.

NOTES

When you're buying fish, be it at a farmers' market or at your local grocery store, don't hesitate to ask your fishmonger to clean and cut your fish for you. When I want to make this stew, I always ask my fishmonger to scale and clean the fish, leaving the head and tail on, and to cut the fish into steaks for me. Also, you can use many varieties of fish for this stew, anything from mackerel to snapper and anything in between.

Bengali Fish and Eggplant Simmer

My mother learned to make this fish stew as a young bride, when my parents lived in a Bengali neighborhood in Calcutta, India, for a few years right after they were married. She generally used *hilsa*, a boney herring that is the national fish of Bangladesh. I loved the flavor of this dish when I was a child, and my mom would stand over me, fearing that I would choke to death on the hilsa's many thin bones. Now, as a mom, I make it with cod fillets, to ease my mind.

The combination of seeds gives this dish its very distinctive flavor. Fenugreek seeds add a subtle, dark, maple-like tinge; the nigella seeds confer an oregano-pepperiness on this stew; and the fennel seeds impart a faint licorice tone. Though often hard to find, it's worth tracking down these particular seed varieties. I think you will find all manner of ways to incorporate them into your cooking.

MAKES 4 SERVINGS

2 teaspoons fenugreek seeds

2 teaspoons nigella seeds

2 teaspoons fennel seeds

6 tablespoons vegetable oil, divided

8 garlic cloves, smashed

4 vine-ripened tomatoes, chopped

2 teaspoons granulated white sugar

3 teaspoons kosher salt, divided

2 cups water

2 pounds cod fillets, cut into
3-inch pieces

2 Japanese eggplants, cut into
thick slices

6 sprigs cilantro

Heat a medium Dutch oven over medium-high heat. Add the seeds to the pan and let them toast for 30 seconds until they pop. Add 1 tablespoon of oil and the garlic, and let the garlic brown for a minute. Add the tomatoes and stir well. Add the sugar and 2 teaspoons of the salt to the tomatoes and let it cook down for 5 minutes on low heat. Add the water and cook for another 10 minutes on low heat. Raise the heat to medium, add the cod to the tomato stew, and cook for about 8 minutes until the fish is cooked through. In the meantime, heat a small skillet with the remaining 5 tablespoons of oil, season the sliced eggplant with the remaining teaspoon of salt, and brown the eggplant on both sides. This should take about 3 to 5 minutes. Remove the sliced eggplant from the pan and transfer the eggplant to the Dutch oven with the fish. Gently stir and let the stew simmer for another 10 minutes or until the eggplant is fully incorporated. Remove from the heat, serve, and garnish with cilantro sprigs.

NOTES

Fennel seeds are usually an easy find. The fenugreek seeds and nigella seeds aren't as readily available in most supermarkets. You'll likely have to find a specialty spice store or an Indian market. Keep in mind that nigella seeds are also known as kalonji *seeds.*

Gooseberry and Watermelon Gazpacho

This salad evolved from having a large, juicy, sweet watermelon in my kitchen one hot summer afternoon. I made myself watermelon ginger juice and, after quenching my thirst with a tall glass of it, I had just a little left over. Next thing you know, that juice found its way into a soup with goose-berries and watercress I had picked up at the farmers' market that morning. Some dishes that have become favorites of mine come from just letting my creative juices flow.

NOTE

If you are having trouble finding gooseberries, seeded scuppernong or muscadine grapes are a good substitute for gooseberries. Rhubarb would work well, too.

MAKES 4 SERVINGS

8 cups chilled seedless watermelon, cut into ½-inch cubes

2 teaspoons grated ginger

1 cup yellow gooseberries, cut in half

2 teaspoons coarsely ground black pepper

2 tablespoons honey

Place 1½ cups of watermelon in each serving bowl. Blend 2 cups of watermelon, along with the ginger, in a blender. Divide the juice equally and pour it into the bowls. Evenly distribute the gooseberries into the bowls. Sprinkle each bowl with the black pepper. Drizzle the honey over the mixture. Serve cold.

Simple School-Night Chicken Pho

One of Ethan's and my favorite things to do is to go to Buford Highway: It is a few-miles-long stretch here in Atlanta that is lined with superb mom-and-pop restaurants that serve some of the best food in Atlanta. When friends visit, I always take them on a "Buford Highway Run," as Ethan and I call it. You can circle the globe by savoring authentic dishes on this culinary field trip.

We go to five or six restaurants and try one specialty dish from each place. It's a fantastic way to spend an afternoon. Nam Phuong Restaurant is our favorite Vietnamese spot. The name roughly translates to "Fragrance of the South," which tugs at my heartstrings.

The pho here is outstanding. But there are nights when I just cannot make myself dive into Atlanta's notoriously snarled traffic. On those nights, I make this simple scaled-down version of pho at home. Just a whole bird cooked down with aromatics and eaten with noodles and fresh herbs.

5 quarts water, divided

1 (2-pound) whole chicken, with giblets removed (but use the neck)

1 large onion with papery skin attached, cut in half

1 head of garlic, skin on, cut in half

1-inch piece of fresh peeled galangal, mashed with a mortar and pestle

1 stalk lemongrass, split in 2

4 Makrut lime leaves

4 star anise

4 teaspoons kosher salt

1 (12-ounce) bottle concentrated chicken-bone broth

1 (14-ounce) bag rice noodles

½ pound bean sprouts

1 small bunch Thai basil

1 small bunch culantro

1 jalapeño sliced

4 key limes, cut in half

1 bunch cilantro, as a garnish

To make the broth: Pour 3 quarts of cold water in a large pot over medium to low heat. Add the whole chicken, onion, garlic, galangal, lemongrass, lime leaves, star anise, and salt to the pot. Let the stock cook for an hour. The liquid should be reduced by one-third at this point. Take the chicken out of the pot and set aside to cool. Pour the broth through a strainer and discard the aromatics. Return the stock to the pot, keep the broth going on low heat, and add the concentrated bone broth. At this point I like to take the chicken off the bone; you can save or discard the chicken skin (in our home we love it). Shred the chicken into big pieces and set aside. Discard the bones.

To prepare the noodles: Soak the noodles for 30 minutes in a large bowl with warm water from the tap. Pour 2 quarts of water in a pot over medium to high heat. When you are ready to serve the pho, blanch the noodles in hot water for 30 seconds to warm them through. Strain the noodles and set aside.

To assemble: Add the noodles to the bowls, along with shredded chicken, pour the broth over each bowl, making sure the noodles are immersed in the soup. Serve the pho with bean sprouts, Thai basil, culantro, jalapeño, lime, and cilantro.

NOTES

Since this is a soup made in a jiffy, I fortify the broth with some concentrated flavor, to mimic the slow-cooked broth found in a longer-cooked pho. Galangal is a rhizome with a citrusy bite that is milder than fresh ginger. Culantro is a tropical herb with long, serrated leaves. It has a stronger flavor than cilantro and holds up well during cooking. If you can't readily get your hand on galangal and culantro, you can substitute ginger and cilantro. You will lose some authentic flavor, but, hey, you won't be stuck in traffic.

Vidalia Onion Soup with Aged Gruyère

Right off the bat, I'm going to tell you this is a process. It is a journey. But in the end, you will be thrilled that you took this trip.

For any French onion soup to be worth its salt, it needs to start with the richest, beefiest, lip-glossing stock. Once that is done, things move at a quick clip. So, first, we are going to roast some meaty soup bones for that depth of flavor that's so important in a soup like this. Then it is all about building the flavors with thyme, bay leaves, and my beloved Tellicherry black pepper. As for the onions, we are going to head three hours south of Atlanta to Vidalia, Georgia, for super-sweet onions. And what would be the point of all of this if we didn't float a hunk of crusty bread in the soup and broil cheese on top until it is nutty and gooey? So settle in, and let's do this. This is enough for six to eight servings, so freeze some or invite everyone over on a chilly night.

MAKES **6 TO 8 SERVINGS**

For the Beef Stock

5 pounds meaty beef bones

2 medium carrots, peeled and roughly chopped

2 stalks celery, roughly chopped

2 medium yellow onions, with papery skin attached, quartered

3 big sprigs of fresh thyme

3 bay leaves

1½ tablespoons Tellicherry black peppercorns

2 tablespoons tomato paste

For the Soup

½ stick (4 tablespoons) unsalted butter, plus 2 tablespoons melted butter for croutons

4 large Vidalia or other sweet onions (about 2 pounds), halved and thinly sliced lengthwise with the grain (about 8 cups)

2 teaspoons kosher salt

¼ teaspoon finely ground Tellicherry black pepper

1 baguette, cut into ½-inch thick rounds

2 quarts beef stock

1 fresh or dry bay leaf

2 cups grated aged Gruyère cheese

To make the beef stock: Heat the oven to 450°F. Roast the bones in a single layer, uncovered in a large roasting pan for 20 minutes. Add the carrots, celery, and the onion quarters with skin attached, and continue roasting until the bones and vegetables are very brown, about 35 to 40 minutes.

Transfer just the bones to a large (5- to 7-quart) stockpot. Add the thyme, bay leaves, peppercorns, and tomato paste. Add enough cold water to the pot to cover the bones by several inches. Bring to a boil over medium heat, reduce the heat to low, and slowly simmer for 4 hours. (Or cook in a large slow cooker, covered, on high for 1 hour, then uncover and cook for 3 more hours.) By this time, the stock should be significantly reduced. Strain the stock into a large container. Let the stock cool before covering and refrigerating. (You can speed up this process by putting the container of stock into a large container filled with ice or adding some freezer cold-packs to the stock.)

Once the stock is chilled, the fat can be removed from the top and saved and used to stir-fry and sauté. Proceed with making the soup now or start again in the next day or two.

To make the soup: Melt the butter in a 4-quart pot or Dutch oven over medium heat. Add the onions and season with salt and pepper. Add ½ cup of the beef stock. Cover and cook for 10 minutes over medium heat. Uncover and increase the heat to high. Cook, occasionally stirring until the stock has evaporated and the onions are browned and tender. Add the remaining beef stock.

Meanwhile, arrange the baguette slices in a single layer on a rimmed baking sheet. Brush with 2 tablespoons of melted butter. Preheat the oven to 350°F. Bake about 15 minutes until the bread is crisp and lightly browned, turning once. Set aside.

Add the broth and bay leaf to the browned onions and bring the soup to a boil over medium-high heat. Reduce the heat to medium-low and simmer for 10 minutes. Discard the bay leaf.

To serve: Position an oven rack 6 inches from the broiler with ample room for your soup bowls to fit. Heat the broiler to high. Put the broilerproof soup bowls or crocks on a rimmed baking sheet. Place 2 or 3 baguette slices in each bowl. Ladle the soup on top. Generously sprinkle each serving with the cheese and broil until the top is browned and bubbly, 2 to 5 minutes. Serve immediately.

CHAPTER FOUR:

vivid vegetables *and* rice dishes

"Color Full" Roasted Vegetables

I am a fool for a colorful platter of roasted vegetables and fruits. I'm also a produce geek: I linger in the produce section and at the farmers' market and just drink in all the colors and textures.

Below are some of my favorite fruit and veggie choices, but feel free to just go wild with your own creative combinations and use this simple, sweet, and savory mix of seasonings to roast up whatever catches your eye. Surely, the bright combination will leave you full.

MAKES 6 SERVINGS

1 small pineapple, skinned and cut into ¼-inch slices

1 large bulb of fennel, cut into ¼-inch slices

2 medium beets, peeled and cut into ¼-inch circles

2 sweet potatoes, peeled and cut into ¼-inch circles

½ pound mini multicolored sweet peppers

6 vine-ripened tomatoes, on the vine

½ cup extra-virgin olive oil

1½ teaspoons kosher salt

2 teaspoons white granulated sugar

2 teaspoons cumin seeds

1 teaspoon black mustard seeds

1 cup Greek yogurt

½ cup honey

Preheat the oven to 400°F. Line two sheet pans with parchment paper, and lay all the fruits and vegetables on the sheet pans. Drizzle the olive oil and sprinkle the salt, sugar, cumin seeds, and mustard seeds evenly over the fruits and vegetables. Place the sheet pans in the oven for 20 to 25 minutes. Remove the pans from the oven. Schmear the Greek yogurt on one end of the serving platter. Place the beets on the yogurt and arrange the rest of the fruits and vegetables on the serving platter. Drizzle with honey and serve. This dish is fantastic warm, or at room temperature.

Three-Mushroom and Bok Choy Stir-Fry

I am a mushroom lover. Whether foraged from the shady woods or purchased from the market, mushrooms always fascinate me. Perhaps I should have been a mycologist. It's not just the deep, earthy flavors of portabellas, the woodsy taste of shiitakes, or the hint of anise in oyster mushrooms; it is also the fanciful shapes I find so appealing. In my mind, the twirling mushrooms look like ballerinas dancing to Tchaikovsky's "Nutcracker Suite," as in the animated film *Fantasia*, when I lay them out on the counter. I just find them magical!

Umami, the "fifth flavor," encompassing savory, is supremely satisfying, and mushrooms are wild with it. Searing bok choy brings that aspect out of this slightly bitter green. When combined with shallots, white pepper, and garlic, then rounded out with butter and oyster sauce, mushrooms and bok choy only need a bed of rice to create an enchanting dinner.

3 tablespoons grapeseed oil

1 bok choy, cut in half lengthwise with stem attached

1 tablespoon unsalted butter

10 garlic cloves, thinly sliced

1 medium shallot, thinly sliced

1 teaspoon ground white pepper

2 tablespoons oyster sauce

½ pound portobello mushrooms, sliced

½ pound shiitake mushrooms, sliced

½ pound thick, meaty, stemmed oyster mushrooms, sliced

Heat a wok on a high heat and add the oil. Once the oil is very hot, sear the bok choy in the wok, flat side facedown, until it is golden brown. This should take no more than a minute. Remove the bok choy from the wok and set aside. Add the butter to the wok. Add the garlic, shallots, and white pepper and cook, stirring for 1 minute until the garlic is a light golden brown. Add the oyster sauce and mix well. Add the mushrooms and cook for 7 minutes, stirring often. Add the bok choy back to the pan and mix well. Cook for another minute. Serve immediately.

NOTES

Don't feel that you have to use only these kinds of mushrooms; there is a world of varieties to choose from. Just be aware of the cooking times: The ones I used here are meatier varieties, so the cooking time on these three are pretty even. If you use any of the more delicate types, be sure to add them later in the stir-frying process.

If you don't have oyster sauce handy, use soy sauce and a touch of molasses to sweeten the soy, which will work equally as well, or try hoisin sauce with a splash of soy.

Lime Leaf and Green Pea Risotto with Fennel

Making risotto puts me in a complete state of Zen. Standing over that pot, stirring continuously, and watching the rice bloom seems to make my troubles slip away. Next thing I know, I just want to curl up on the couch with a warm bowl of risotto and a glass of white burgundy, and get caught up on my Netflix shows.

MAKES **4 SERVINGS**

2 tablespoons olive oil

2 tablespoons unsalted butter

1 cup Vidalia onions, chopped

1 cup chopped fennel

2 garlic cloves, finely chopped

4 Makrut lime leaves

2 cups Arborio rice

2 tablespoons lime juice

1 cup dry white wine

6 cups chicken broth, divided

⅔ cup grated Parmesan cheese

1 cup fresh or frozen green sweet peas, thawed

½ cup chopped fennel fronds

Heat a pan with the olive oil and butter on medium-high. Add the onions, fennel, and garlic.

Cook, stirring occasionally, for 5 to 6 minutes or until tender. Add the lime leaves. Add the rice and mix well, so the rice is well coated. Add the lime juice and wine, and simmer over low heat, continually stirring until all the wine is absorbed, about 5 minutes. Add 2 cups of the broth and continuously stir until the broth is absorbed, about 10 minutes. Continue doing this with the rest of the broth. The whole process should take about 20 minutes of constant stirring. Add the cheese and stir well. Add the peas and stir well. Turn off the heat. I like the peas to just be warmed through and cooked with the residual heat. Add the fennel fronds and stir. Serve warm.

Grilled Meyer Lemon Chili Corn

Grilled corn is one of those dishes that takes me right back to my childhood. We lived in the north of India, in a state called Gujrat, for two summers when I was 11 years old. Bushels of fresh corn would show up at our doorstep during the summer months. Fresh, sweet corn on open flames, rubbed with lemon, sprinkled with chili and salt, all my brothers and cousins running around in the front yard on hot summer afternoons, drinking mango lassi and eating corn on the cob. Splendid, sweet memories!

MAKES 4 SERVINGS

4 ears of corn, with the husk attached and silk removed

2 Meyer lemons

½ teaspoon chili powder

½ teaspoon kosher salt

Place the corn on the grill 4 to 6 inches above medium heat and make sure you get a nice char all around the whole corn. You have to keep turning the corn on the grill to make sure it's not getting burned. This should take no more than 5 to 7 minutes. Remove from the grill and rub the Meyer lemon all over the corn. Sprinkle with the chili powder and salt, and chomp away.

NOTE

I like to braid the corn husks to make a handle for easy eating, and it looks so pretty, too.

Dill and Red-Onion Rice

I believe that rice can be the start of a meal and doesn't always have to play second fiddle. Here's one of my favorite rice recipes. Dill and cumin come together quite harmoniously with fragrant rice and gently browned red onion.

MAKES 4 SERVINGS

2 tablespoons ghee or unsalted clarified butter

1 medium red onion, halved and thinly sliced

2 teaspoons cumin seeds

1½ cups basmati rice

2 cups water

1 cup coconut milk

2 teaspoons kosher salt

1 cup chopped fresh dill, divided

¼ cup pomegranate seeds, for garnish

Heat a small pot over medium heat, add the ghee, the onions, and cumin, and cook, stirring occasionally for 3 minutes or until the onions are golden brown. Add the rice, water, coconut milk, and salt, along with ⅓ cup of the dill. Bring the water to a boil. Lower the heat and cover. Cook for 10 minutes and then turn the heat off. Do not open the lid for 5 minutes, the residual heat will finish the cooking process. Lift the lid, add the rest of the dill, and fluff up the rice with a fork. Serve warm. Garnish with pomegranate seeds.

NOTES
If you'd like to be a little bit more decadent, sauté some black currants and golden raisins in a little bit of ghee and fold them into the rice. Just about any type of rice works well in this recipe.

Greek Briam

Briam is the Grecian way of roasting vegetables. Potatoes and carrots give this dish enough substance to serve as the main course and yellow squash, zucchini, and tomatoes pair well as a side for just about anything. This is one of those clean-out-the-fridge recipes, so sometimes I'll throw in some eggplant slices and shaved fennel. Serve this as a one-dish dinner or alongside some warm, puffy pita.

MAKES 4 SERVINGS

1 (32-ounce) can diced tomatoes, divided

6 garlic cloves, thinly sliced

3 teaspoons kosher salt, divided

1 tablespoon fresh oregano

1 teaspoon crushed chili flakes

1 medium red onion, halved and thinly sliced

1 large carrot, thinly sliced

2 medium red bliss potatoes, thinly sliced

1 large yellow squash, thinly sliced

1 large zucchini, thinly sliced

¼ cup extra-virgin olive oil

½ cup chopped fresh tarragon

8 ounces crumbled feta

Preheat the oven to 425°F. Pour two-thirds of the diced tomatoes into a cast-iron skillet. Add the garlic slices to the tomatoes. Evenly sprinkle 1 teaspoon of kosher salt, oregano, and crushed chili flakes over the diced tomatoes. In a separate pan, toss the vegetables with the olive oil and 2 teaspoons of salt, then transfer the vegetables to the cast-iron skillet. Pour the remaining tomatoes over the vegetables and place them in the oven for 25 minutes. Remove from the oven and serve warm with chopped fresh tarragon and crumbled feta.

NOTE

This is a recipe where springing for excellent extra-virgin olive oil really makes a difference because the potatoes will lap it up.

Gorgonzola Three-Potato Gratin

Let's face it: Potatoes are often the bland accompaniment to the main attraction. What I want instead is a sock-you-in-the-face, cheesy, decadent dish that can hold its own for lunch or a light dinner with a salad. I suggest a glass of pinot bianco if you're going the salad route and a heady cabernet if you're pairing this with the Spice-Rubbed Rib-Eye Steaks (page 159).

MAKES **6 TO 8 SERVINGS**

2 tablespoons salted butter, softened, divided

1½ cups crumbled gorgonzola cheese, divided

2 cups half-and-half

1 teaspoon kosher salt

2 garlic cloves, smashed

Generous grating of whole nutmeg

½ pound Yukon Gold potatoes, very thinly sliced

½ pound red bliss potatoes, very thinly sliced

½ pound purple potatoes, very thinly sliced

Butter a 9 by 13-inch baking dish with 1 tablespoon of the butter and sprinkle with ¼ cup of the cheese. In a large pot, bring the half-and-half to a boil over medium-high heat. Add the kosher salt, smashed garlic, and nutmeg. Add the sliced potatoes. Return to a boil then reduce heat to medium-low and simmer for 8 to 10 minutes or until the potatoes are tender.

Preheat the oven to 350°F. With a slotted spoon, move half the potatoes to the buttered dish. Arrange the potatoes in an even layer. Sprinkle half the remaining cheese over the potatoes. Spoon the rest of the potatoes over the cheese layer and top with the remaining cheese. Pour the hot, seasoned half-and-half over the potatoes. Bake for 40 to 45 minutes or until bubbly and the cheese is lightly browned. Remove from the oven and let settle for at least 10 minutes before serving.

Seed-Crusted Whole Roasted Cauliflower

If you like to entertain, as I do, then astonish your guests with this brined, whole roasted cauliflower. Seriously, it looks pretty fantastic on the table.

The cauliflower gets dolled up for the party. First, it is briefly boiled in its brine. Then it gets a coating of garlic-flavored yogurt and dressed with flaky sea salt, poppy seeds, and sesame seeds. A spritz of olive oil holds the seed coating in place. This is an elegant dinner party addition and would be superb for New Year's Eve.

MAKES 4 SERVINGS

1 large head of cauliflower, stem and leaves attached

1½ teaspoons kosher salt

1 tablespoon granulated white sugar

4 garlic cloves, mashed

1 cup yogurt

1 tablespoon poppy seeds

1 tablespoon sesame seeds

1 tablespoon black sesame seeds

1 teaspoon flaky sea salt

Olive oil spray

To brine the cauliflower: Place enough water in a large pot to cover the cauliflower, add 1½ teaspoons kosher salt and 1 tablespoon sugar, and let the cauliflower soak overnight.

To ensure that the cauliflower cooks through. I like to boil it for 10 minutes, in the same pot that it soaked in overnight. Remove from the water and let it cool until it's safe enough to handle. Pat dry.

Preheat the oven to 350°F. Place the cauliflower in a cast-iron skillet. Mash the garlic cloves in a mortar and pestle. Mix the mashed garlic with the yogurt, then evenly spread the yogurt all over the cauliflower. Mix the poppy seeds, sesame seeds, black sesame seeds, and flaky sea salt in a small bowl and sprinkle them evenly over the yogurt on the cauliflower. Generously spray the olive oil evenly on the seed-coated cauliflower. Roast the cauliflower for 30 minutes or until the seeds are toasted, and the yogurt is slightly browned.

Roasted Butternut Squash with Tomato-Ginger Gravy

A couple of nights a week, there's usually a sheet pan in my oven, lined with parchment paper and stacked with vegetables drizzled with olive oil, slathered with honey, and sprinkled with spices. I love making a meal this way. One pan to wash? I'm sold! This hearty squash in a fresh tomato puree, cooked down with caramelized ginger, makes for a perfect sheet-pan meal. It's simple and delicious all at once.

MAKES 4 SERVINGS

4 small butternut squash

4 tablespoons unsalted butter, divided

4 tablespoons honey

2 teaspoons coarsely ground black pepper

1½ teaspoons pink Himalayan salt, divided

2 tablespoons olive oil

2 tablespoons fresh ginger, peeled and finely grated

6 fresh plum tomatoes, pureed

2 teaspoons light brown sugar

1 tablespoon finely chopped fresh oregano leaves

Preheat the oven to 400°F. Line a sheet pan with parchment paper. Cut the butternut squash in half lengthwise from the stem down. I like leaving the stem and skin on for this recipe. Use a small spoon to scoop the seeds out. Using a paring knife, score the flesh side of the butternut squash horizontally and then vertically. Place the butternut squash on the sheet pan, skin-side down. Rub each half of the butternut squash with 1½ teaspoons of the butter. Drizzle the honey evenly all over the butternut squash and season them with the black pepper and 1 teaspoon of salt. Place the pan in the oven and roast for 20 to 25 minutes or until the butternut squash is fork-tender.

In the meantime, make the tomato gravy. Place a small pan over medium heat. Add the olive oil and ginger. Cook the ginger for 2 to 3 minutes until golden brown. Add the fresh tomato puree to the ginger. Stir in the brown sugar and the remaining ½ teaspoon of salt. Let the tomatoes cook down and reduce by half; this should take about 15 minutes. Serve the tomato gravy alongside the roasted butternut squash. Garnish with fresh oregano.

Persian Fesenjan Chickpeas with Spinach

I've always loved Persian flavors. From the time I lived in New York City when I first came to the States, to making my home here in Georgia, I've sought out Persian restaurants and markets. Here in Atlanta, I trek out to Roswell to go to Shahrzad, the Persian Market; it's my spot for dried nuts and fruits. There I buy the raw walnuts and pomegranate molasses to make my fesenjan. It's such a uniquely flavored dish—tangy and sweet with beautiful hints of cinnamon and nutmeg. I hope you enjoy this dish as much as I do. I encourage you to serve it with Dill and Red-Onion Rice (page 74)

2 cups walnuts

3 tablespoons vegetable oil

1 large yellow onion, diced

4 garlic cloves, finely chopped

2 teaspoons turmeric powder

1 teaspoon coarsely ground black pepper

1 teaspoon cumin seeds

½ teaspoon freshly grated nutmeg

2 cinnamon sticks

2 tablespoons light brown sugar

1½ teaspoons kosher salt

Orange zest (2 to 3 wide strips of zest)

2 cups chicken stock

¼ cup pomegranate molasses

1 (28-ounce) can chickpeas, drained

4 cups torn fresh spinach leaves

Preheat the oven to 400°F. Spread the walnuts on a sheet pan and place in the oven for 5 minutes. Remove them from the oven and let them cool, then pulse the walnuts in a food processor.

Heat the oil in a Dutch oven over medium-high heat. Add the onions and cook, stirring occasionally for 4 to 5 minutes or until the onions are golden brown. Add the garlic and cook for about 1 minute or until it just begins to brown. Add the turmeric, pepper, cumin, nutmeg, and cinnamon, and let the spices roast for a minute. Add the brown sugar and salt, and give it a quick stir. Add the orange zest, stock, pomegranate molasses, and walnuts, and simmer for 2 minutes, stirring well until everything is incorporated. Lower the heat to medium-low and add the chickpeas. Cover the Dutch oven with a lid and cook for 20 minutes. Remove the lid and cook for another 5 minutes until the sauce is nice and thick. Remove from the heat and fold in the spinach.

NOTE

If you can't find pomegranate molasses, buy pomegranate juice and cook down 1½ cups of juice to ½ cup. This should take about 25 minutes on medium-low heat. You're looking for a nice, thick syrup consistency. Use less sugar than I call for if you'd like it more savory and tangy.

Japanese Eggplant with Peanut Sauce

I'm that person! The eggplant lover. I also love a satay sauce. This sauce is a perfect balance of sweet, salt, heat, tartness, and nuttiness. This eggplant dish is a wonderful choice if you are trending flexitarian. Try the sauce with skewers of grilled vegetables, shrimp, or chicken. Heck, put it on just about anything that needs a little livening up.

MAKES 4 SERVINGS

½ cup unsalted peanuts (no skin)

1 tablespoon chopped lemongrass

1 tablespoon finely chopped galangal

2 garlic cloves

1 small shallot, peeled

1 tablespoon lime juice

Zest of 1 lime

1 tablespoon light brown sugar

1 tablespoon fish sauce

1 teaspoon turmeric powder

1 teaspoon kosher salt

⅓ cup water

8 small Japanese eggplants, halved lengthwise

5 tablespoons vegetable oil, divided

1 teaspoon chili flakes

Reserve a few peanuts, to make about a tablespoon of crushed peanuts for the garnish. Place the remaining peanuts, along with the lemongrass, galangal, garlic, shallots, lime juice and zest, brown sugar, fish sauce, turmeric, salt, and water in a food processor, and pulse to make a coarse paste. Transfer the sauce to a small pot and warm over low heat for 10 minutes.

Score the eggplants by cutting shallow crosshatching across the flesh. Preheat the oven to 400°F. Line a sheet pan with parchment paper. Place the eggplants on the pan. Drizzle 3 tablespoons of the oil and drizzle a few sprigs evenly over the eggplant. Place the pan in the oven and roast for 20 minutes. Remove from the oven and set aside.

Heat a small skillet over medium heat with the remaining 2 tablespoons of oil.

Add the chili flakes to the oil and let them bloom for 30 seconds.

Pour the tempered chili oil over the eggplants and serve warm, along with the peanut sauce.

CHAPTER FIVE:

splendid seafood

Passion Fruit, Lime, and Grapefruit Grouper Ceviche

On a trip to Lima, Peru, I ate ceviche every day. I was there with CARE (Cooperative for Assistance and Relief Everywhere) meeting with local farmers who had participated in our programs there. My job was to listen to their stories firsthand so I could come back and lobby the United States Congress on CARE's behalf and stress the importance of funding those programs.

I always assumed that ceviche meant that the fish was marinated in lime or lemon juice. I discovered that any sour, acidic agent makes an excellent ceviche. I have tried varieties made with bitter oranges, passion fruit, tiger's milk, and tamarind—all eye-opening and delicious.

Search for finger hot chilies to add to this tropical ceviche. Serrano chilies make a suitable substitution.

MAKES 4 SERVINGS

⅓ cup fresh lime juice

¼ cup fresh, ripe, passion fruit pulp

2 finger hot chilies, seeded and finely chopped

1 tablespoon cane syrup

1 teaspoon pink Himalayan salt

1 teaspoon crushed red pepper flakes

1 pound grouper, skin and bones removed, cut into 1-inch pieces

10 cherry tomatoes, quartered

¼ cup finely diced sweet mango

2 small grapefruits, segmented

¼ cup fresh cilantro leaves

½ teaspoon coarsely ground black pepper

In a medium bowl, make a marinade by mixing together the lime juice, passion fruit pulp, chilies, cane syrup, salt, and red pepper flakes. Toss the fish with the marinade and let it sit for at least 10 minutes, or up to 2 hours. Add the tomatoes, mango, grapefruit, and cilantro leaves. Sprinkle with black pepper. Transfer to a platter and serve.

Caribbean Fried Snapper

The Caribbean islands remind me of the beaches of my childhood in Kerala. But it is not just the sun, sand, and crystal waters I adore. It is also the flavors—spiceforward, seafood with a peppery punch, and a balance of tart and sweet make me feel entirely at home in the islands. I have visited St. Croix, St. Thomas, St. Lucia, Jamaica, Antigua, and Puerto Rico. When I am longing for a trip to the sunny, sandy beaches, I make this lightly fried fish, swimming in pickled pepper sauce.

1 tablespoon hot paprika

1 tablespoon garlic powder

½ tablespoon onion powder

3 teaspoons coarsely ground black pepper

3 teaspoons kosher salt

3 (2-pound) snappers, cleaned, scaled, and scored, fish and tail on

2 cups vegetable oil

1 cup white vinegar

2 tablespoons granulated white sugar

1 teaspoon kosher salt

10 whole allspice berries

1 small Scotch bonnet pepper, thinly sliced

1 medium yellow onion, cut into thin circles

1 medium carrot, peeled and thinly sliced

1 small red bell pepper, thinly sliced

1 small green bell pepper, thinly sliced

In a small bowl, mix the paprika, garlic powder, onion powder, black pepper, and salt into a dry rub. Season the fish with this spice rub and let it sit for an hour in the refrigerator.

In a large frying pan, heat the oil on medium heat. Add the snapper to the hot oil and fry for 8 minutes until it's golden brown on one side, then flip the fish over with a slotted fish spatula. Cook for another 8 minutes. Remove from the oil and set the fish aside on a serving plate.

In a separate medium skillet, heat the vinegar, sugar, salt, allspice, and Scotch bonnet pepper on medium heat. Add the onions, carrots, and peppers, and cook for 2 to 3 minutes, until the mixture is heated through. Remove from the heat and pour the vinegar mixture and quick-pickled vegetables over the fried snapper. Serve immediately.

NOTES

The Scotch bonnet pepper is one of the hottest peppers, and I highly recommend wearing gloves when handling it. I also highly recommend turning on the vent above the stove when preparing the sauce because it can get pretty intense when those peppers and vinegar start bubbling.

Steelhead Trout Poke Bowl

My son, Ethan, loves a poke bowl. I'm thrilled that he finds the servings of fresh fish, vegetables, and rice satisfying. When I pick him up from school, if I haven't cooked dinner at home, we pop by one of our favorite haunts, DUB's Fishcamp, my dear friend Anne Quatrano's restaurant in Ponce City Market. Ninety percent of the time Ethan will order the poke bowl there. So I decided to learn how to make it at home and, every now and then, when he gets home from school, I'll have this waiting for a very, very, very, hungry young man. He ends up being a very full and content young man.

MAKES 4 SERVINGS

For the Sushi Rice

2 cups short grained sushi rice

2 cups water

2 tablespoons rice vinegar

1 tablespoon granulated white sugar

2 teaspoons kosher salt

For the Trout

1½ pounds skinless steelhead trout, filleted, and cut into ½-inch pieces

½ cup teriyaki sauce

2 teaspoons sesame oil

1 teaspoon Korean chili flakes

For the Scallion Vinaigrette

1 tablespoon soy sauce

1 tablespoon honey

2 tablespoons grapeseed oil

1 whole scallion, thinly sliced

1 teaspoon finely chopped ginger

1 teaspoon finely chopped garlic

1 teaspoon toasted sesame seeds

1 Hass avocado, cut into ½ inch pieces

To make the sushi rice: Rinse the rice well. In a medium pot over medium-high heat, place the rice and 2 cups water, and stir well. Bring the water to a boil. Reduce the heat to low and cover the pot with a lid. Cook for 10 minutes. Remove from the heat and let the rice stay covered for 10 more minutes. In a small bowl, mix the rice vinegar, sugar, and salt. Transfer the rice to a glass bowl and fold in the rice vinegar mixture, so it's well incorporated. Let the rice cool to room temperature.

To prepare the steelhead trout: In a glass bowl, lightly toss the steelhead trout, teriyaki sauce, sesame oil, and Korean chili flakes and let it sit for 10 minutes.

To make the scallion vinaigrette: In a small bowl, whisk the soy sauce, honey, and grapeseed oil together. Add the scallions, ginger, garlic, and toasted sesame seeds, and mix well.

To assemble: Distribute the rice evenly into 4 bowls. Top the rice with the steelhead trout, and fresh avocado. Finish with the scallion vinaigrette.

Deep-Fried Whole Smelt Bhajia

Most of us learned really early in life that when you drench something in batter and deep-fry it, it's going to be delicious.

I've eaten small, whole, battered fried fish in Italy, Spain, Greece, and all up and down the American coasts. This fried smelt bhajia is a culmination of my mother's kitchen and many other kitchens around the world. These get a quick dip in a chickpea-and-rice flour batter, then are fried up in a flash.

MAKES 4 SERVINGS

½ cup chickpea flour

2 tablespoons rice flour

1 teaspoon chili powder

1 teaspoon turmeric

2 teaspoons onion powder

1 teaspoon dried fenugreek leaves

1 teaspoon kosher salt

½ cup water

2 cups vegetable oil, for frying

1 pound smelt, cleaned

To make the batter, mix together in a bowl all the ingredients, except the oil and the fish. The batter should be the consistency of pancake batter. Place the oil in a frying pan over medium-high heat. When the oil is hot (to check if the oil is hot, I usually drop a tiny amount of batter in the oil; if the batter rises up to the top, the oil is ready), dip the fish in the batter and drop the fish in the oil. Fry for 3 to 4 minutes until the batter is golden brown. Using a slotted spoon, remove the fish from the oil and place on a plate, lined with paper towels. Serve warm.

NOTES

Small fish like smelt and sardines are not the easiest to find in my local grocery stores and markets. They are seasonal, and you have to keep an eye out for them and snag them when you see them.

If you can't get your hand on fenugreek leaves, use ½ teaspoon dried oregano and ½ teaspoon dried parsley instead.

Asha's Fish Fry

If you were to ask me what I'd like my last meal to be, I'd say masala-rubbed fried fish.

It reminds me of my mother, my birthplace, the beaches I roamed as a child, and my ancestors. When I go, I'd like to leave remembering the people, the flavors, and the land that molded me and allowed me to become the woman of the world I became. This turmeric and lime fish is on heavy rotation at my home because it doesn't take much effort to get a fantastic meal on the table. It's excellent paired with greens or boiled yucca. If it were my last meal, I'd have it with Yellow Split Pea Sambar with Turnips, Eggplant, and Butternut Squash (page 50) and simple, steamed rice.

MAKES 4 SERVINGS

4 teaspoons hot paprika

4 teaspoons garlic powder

2 teaspoons coarsely ground pepper

1 teaspoon turmeric powder

1 teaspoon kosher salt

4 tablespoons fresh lime juice

2 tablespoons water, if needed

4 (⅓-pound) kingfish steaks

1 cup vegetable oil, for frying

In a bowl mix, all the spices, salt, and lime juice. Add the water, as required, for the rub to be a pasty consistency. Massage the rub on the fish and let it sit for an hour in the refrigerator. Heat the oil in a medium skillet over medium heat. Add the spice-rubbed kingfish steaks, let them cook for about 4 minutes on one side, then flip them over and cook them for another 4 minutes on the other side or until the fish is just cooked through. Remove from the pan and serve immediately.

NOTES

I like to use kingfish steaks when I make this dish. If you've never had kingfish or king mackerel before, I hope you try it! Kingfish is a steaky, white-flesh fish, a bit softer to the touch and on the palate than tuna or swordfish. Spanish mackerel may be easier to find and works perfectly well in this recipe.

Ginger-Scallion Steamed Branzino

Branzino is also called Mediterranean Sea Bass, a lush, silver-skinned, tender white fish that's terrific when steamed. It's available either wild-caught or farm-raised, but, either way, it is one of the best choices of sustainable fish.

You will need a steamer basket large enough to hold the fish and a pot to place the basket into while it cooks. This dish is dramatic when served at the table. Splashing the hot oil over the tender poached fish always brings oos and ahhs, when it sizzles and aromatic steam wafts over the table, enchanting guests.

MAKES 2 SERVINGS

2 quarts water

2 medium (¾-pound) Branzino, cleaned, with head on

1 teaspoon crushed black pepper

1 teaspoon kosher salt

1 strip of banana leaf to line the steamer, or parchment paper

¼ cup vegetable oil

2-inch piece of ginger, peeled and thinly sliced

3 scallions, thinly sliced

¼ cup light soy sauce

cilantro, for garnish

Bring the water to a boil in a pot with a lid beneath a steamer basket. Season the fish with the pepper and salt (make sure you season the cavities as well). Place the banana leaf on the steamer, making sure the leaf is not too broad and is not covering the entire base. The idea is to have the leaf directly under the fish, to make it easier to transfer the fish to a serving platter. Place the fish on the banana leaf in the steamer, cover, and cook for 8 minutes or until the fish is just cooked through. In the meantime, heat the oil in a small skillet. When the fish is done, using the banana leaf or parchment paper, transfer the fish to a heat-resistant platter.

Place the ginger, scallions, and cilantro over the fish, and pour the hot oil over the fish and the aromatics. Immediately pour the soy sauce over the fish and serve.

NOTE

Any flaky white fish, like snapper or flounder, would also work great for this dish. Speak to your fishmonger and have them scale and clean your fish for you. I like to leave the head on, you can opt not to do so if it freaks you out. But you will miss out on some delicious morsels.

Fire-Roasted Mackerel

At my culinary clubhouse Third Space, I have a visiting chef series, where I invite friends from all over the world to come cook with me. This recipe came to fruition when my friend Xavier Pacheco visited me from Puerto Rico. Boy, did we have a blast at that dinner—imagine Puerto Rico meeting Indian flavors. It was definitely a night to remember.

We swathed whole mackerels with a paste made of cilantro, jalapeño, and garlic, then blanketed them with coriander, chili powder, and turmeric. After a brief char over hot coals, we roasted them, then squeezed lemon over the steaming fish just before serving. There were smiles all around that night. These fish are beautiful when presented at the table and are sure to garner smiles when you serve them.

For this recipe, the open fire is just to get the smoke and char on the fish. You don't want to let the spices burn, which would make for a bitter-tasting fish. Finishing it in the oven keeps the flavors of the spices and fish intact. But if you happen to have plenty of room on your grill, move them well away from the flame and finish cooking them over indirect heat, drizzle the fish with oil, and let them finish cooking. My grill just isn't big enough to hold enough fish, so I always use the oven at Third Space.

While the grill is hot and the fish is roasting in the oven, throw some tomatoes and onions, to char, over the flames to serve alongside this smoky fish.

MAKES 4 SERVINGS

4 (8-ounce) whole mackerel, head and tail on

2 cups cilantro leaves and stems, roughly chopped

6 tablespoons vegetable oil, divided

2 tablespoons fresh lemon juice

1 jalapeño pepper

4 garlic cloves

1 teaspoon kosher salt

1 teaspoon chili powder

1 teaspoon coriander powder

2 teaspoons turmeric powder

2 lemons, cut in half

Pat the fish dry with paper towels and set aside. In a blender, combine the cilantro, 2 tablespoons of the vegetable oil, lemon juice, jalapeño pepper, garlic, and salt. Blend until the mixture is a coarse paste (the consistency of a chimichurri sauce). Apply this mixture generously to the fish inside and all over the skin. Sprinkle the mackerel all over with the chili powder, coriander powder, and turmeric powder.

Preheat the oven to 400°F. Heat the grill to medium-high. Place the mackerel 6 to 8 inches over medium-high heat and get a nice char on both sides, about 2 to 3 minutes on each side, often turning to prevent the spices from burning. Move the mackerel to a sheet pan and drizzle with the remaining oil. Roast in the oven for 10 to 12 minutes. Remove from the oven, squeeze fresh lemon juice on the fish, and serve at once.

NOTE

Check out Xavier's interview with Anthony Bourdain on the Parts Unknown *episode titled "Life After Maria" to get an idea of what a special person he is.*

Catalonian Paella

I've come to realize that travel is the most beautiful gift I will ever give my child. The life lessons he learns visiting different countries are lessons he would rarely ever learn in a classroom. It has broadened his worldview and made him a more empathetic human being. Every country we visit becomes an indelible lesson about art, architecture, landscapes, and, most importantly, people and their culture. We always bring back a souvenir recipe or two. The memories and friendships shared over meals become a part of our home. From Barcelona, we brought back this recipe for golden, seafood-studded Catalonian paella. It is one of the best recipes for festive gatherings and special occasions where the company and sharing stories of adventures are as important as the meal.

MAKES 8 SERVINGS

½ cup olive oil

16 large prawns or jumbo shrimp, deveined, shell and head on

3 teaspoons kosher salt, divided

2 teaspoons coarsely ground black pepper, divided

2 teaspoons smoked paprika, divided

1 large yellow onion, thinly sliced

2 red bell peppers, seeded and cut into thin strips

10 garlic cloves, finely chopped

1 large tomato, thinly sliced

2 cups yellow Spanish rice mix

8 cups shrimp stock or low-sodium chicken stock

1 pound mussels, debearded

1 pound little neck clams

½ pound baby squid, with tentacles

¼ pound fresh or frozen green peas

2 lemons, cut into wedges

½ cup chopped flat-leaf parsley

Heat the oil on high heat in a large paella pan. Season the prawns with ½ teaspoon salt, ½ teaspoon pepper, and ½ teaspoon smoked paprika. Sear the prawns in the pan, 1 minute on each side, then remove from pan and set aside.

Add the onions, red peppers, garlic, and ½ teaspoon each salt, black pepper, and smoked paprika, and cook for 3 minutes, stirring often until the onions are translucent. Add the tomatoes and cook for another 3 minutes until all of it is well incorporated. This is your sofrito, which will flavor the rice. Add the rice and mix well. Add 4 cups of the stock, and place on low heat. Add 1 teaspoon of salt and mix well. Keep stirring the rice. Since we are cooking this dish with and without a lid, you have to be patient and watch the rice closely. Stir often. As the liquid starts evaporating, slowly keep adding the remainder of the stock. Cover the pot and cook for 10 minutes. Then remove the lid and continue to cook for another 10 minutes or so. When the rice is al dente, and there is still some liquid in the pan, add the mussels, clams, and squid to the pan. The mussels and clams should open up in 5 minutes or less. Place the prawns back in the pan, add the peas and cook for another 2 minutes. Serve immediately with a lemon wedge and garnish with parsley.

NOTES

Sofrito is the base for a lot of rice dishes in Latin and Spanish cooking—it is generally made with onions, peppers, tomatoes, and spices. If you don't have a paella pan, use a very large sauté pan or a substantial cast-iron skillet. You can also halve this recipe and cook it in two pans. That way one can be placed at each end of a long table.

Blackened Catfish Taco

We can thank the late, great chef Paul Prudhomme for setting off a firestorm of blackened fish and seafood dishes, inspired by his blending of creole and Cajun techniques and flavors.

For this blackened catfish taco, I make the seasoning at home, and it holds up well to this high-heat method for cooking fish. And I'm giving you a strong forewarning: Make sure you have a window or two and maybe even the back door open in your home and your vent hood set on high when blackening the catfish. It's going to get smoky! Or make the fish outside on a portable burner or in a skillet, set on a hot grill.

For the Slaw

1 cup thinly sliced carrots strips

1 cup thinly sliced purple cabbage

¼ cup fresh parsley, chopped

2 garlic cloves, finely chopped

1 tablespoon lime juice

1 tablespoon honey

2 tablespoons olive oil

1 teaspoon crushed cumin seeds

½ teaspoon kosher salt

For the Spice Blend

2 teaspoons fresh, coarsely ground black pepper

2 teaspoons chili powder

2 teaspoons celery seeds

2 teaspoons dried thyme

2 teaspoons dried oregano

1 tablespoon sweet paprika

1 tablespoon garlic powder

1½ teaspoons kosher salt

For the Tacos

1 stick (8 tablespoons) melted unsalted butter

2 pounds catfish fillets cut into 2-inch wide strips

1 tablespoon vegetable oil

1 dozen fresh small corn tortillas

Lemon wedges, for serving

To make the slaw: Mix the carrots, purple cabbage, and parsley in a bowl. In a small bowl, whisk the garlic, lime juice, honey, olive oil, cumin, and salt. Pour the dressing over the carrots, cabbage, and parsley. Toss and set aside.

To make the spice blend: In a large bowl, mix all the dry spices together.

To make the tacos: Place the melted butter in a bowl and dip the catfish pieces in the butter before placing them in the bowl with the spices. Toss all the catfish pieces in the spice mixture. Heat a large cast-iron skillet over high heat. Let the cast-iron skillet heat for 2 to 3 minutes. Coat the cast-iron skillet with a tablespoon of vegetable oil. Place the catfish pieces in the cast-iron skillet (don't crowd the pieces in the skillet; make sure you have enough room to flip them). Let the fish pieces cook for 2 minutes and then, using a fish spatula, flip the fish and let them cook for 2 minutes before you remove them from the skillet. Repeat until all the fish is cooked.

To serve: Place a few pieces of the catfish, along with the slaw, on each tortilla, squeeze a lemon wedge over each, and serve.

NOTE

For the best, cleanest-tasting catfish, be sure to look for US Farm-Raised. I'm partial to Simmons Catfish, shipped fresh from Yazoo City, Mississippi.

Tender Squid with Curry Leaves and Fresh Grated Coconut

I come from a tradition in India where we ate with our hands for the most part. Even today, if I make my mother's fish curry and rice, you'd better believe I'm eating with my hands. One childhood memory that lingers around squid, in particular, is that I would wear the rounds of squid as rings, and eat them right off my fingers.

This recipe may seem to call for a long time to cook the squid, because squid usually cooks up in under 5 minutes. For this recipe, however, cooking it for a more extended period gives it the flavor. The squid cooks up fast, then gets tough, and then, the longer it cooks, the more it breaks down to become tender again. Also, note that the squid will end up shrinking down to about half its original size.

MAKES 4 SERVINGS

3 pounds squid, with rings and tentacles

2 cups fresh or frozen grated coconut

1 serrano pepper

6 garlic cloves

2 teaspoons cumin seeds

2 teaspoons turmeric powder

¾ teaspoon kosher salt

2 tablespoons coconut oil

½ teaspoon black mustard seeds

2 small shallots, thinly sliced

2 sprigs curry leaves, about 10 to 12 leaves

Clean and rinse the squid and let it sit in a colander for 10 minutes to drain out all the excess water. Place the grated coconut, serrano pepper, garlic, cumin seeds, turmeric, and salt in a food processor with the blade attachment, and pulse until everything is well incorporated.

Heat a large wok or a large skillet over medium-high heat. Add the coconut oil.

Add the mustard seeds and let the mustard seeds pop, about 1 minute. Add the shallots and curry leaves and cook until the shallots are golden brown for about 3 minutes. Add the squid and the grated coconut mixture, mix well, and cook for 20 minutes, often stirring until all the liquid has evaporated, and you're left with just the squid, coated with the grated coconut. Remove from the heat and serve.

Tandoori Masala Crawfish Boil

I live in the South, and we do love a seafood boil in these parts. Both Cajun and Low Country styles just holler, "Time to party!" I make my seafood boil with a tandoori spice masala. It's a fantastic twist on a seafood boil. Folks will be rolling up their sleeves and digging into these spiced "mudbugs," dripping in well-seasoned butter.

MAKES **6 SERVINGS**

For the Tandoori Masala

4 tablespoons Kashmiri chili powder

2 tablespoons ground coriander

2 tablespoons ground cumin

1 tablespoon coarsely ground black pepper

2 tablespoons salt

1 tablespoon granulated white sugar

2 teaspoons ground ginger

2 teaspoons cardamom powder

2 teaspoons ground cinnamon

2 teaspoons saffron threads

For the Butter Sauce

1½ sticks (12 tablespoons) unsalted butter, melted

1 tablespoon lemon juice

1½ teaspoons lemon zest

2 garlic cloves, finely chopped

1 tablespoon tandoori masala

For the Boil

6 quarts water

½ cup tandoori masala

1 stick (8 tablespoons) unsalted butter, divided

4 pounds crawfish, preferably live or frozen in shell

1 teaspoon coarsely ground black pepper

To make the Tandooori Masala: Mix all of the spices together.

To make the butter sauce: In a small saucepan, melt the butter with the lemon juice, zest, garlic, and tandoori masala over low heat. Keep warm while boiling the crawfish.

To make the boil: In a stockpot, bring the water, the tandoori masala, and the butter to a boil on high heat. Add the crawfish and cook for 6 to 8 minutes. Remove from heat and strain the liquid. Toss the crawfish in half the butter sauce, sprinkle with the pepper, and serve the other half of the butter sauce alongside it for dipping.

NOTE

Store any remaining tandoori masala in an air tight container. This spice blend is also wonderful on grilled chicken or fish.

Spicy Garlic Shrimp with Capers

When I spent my college years in New York City, each weeknight was a food adventure, from India Town to Chinatown, Little Italy, and beyond. I remember stumbling onto this quaint little Italian restaurant, and every time I had a craving for Italian, I'd find my way there. I believe it was over on Mulberry Street. The name escapes me after all these years. What hasn't left me was the warm service with seasoned servers, who spoke Italian, and their spicy shrimp marinara over linguini. Over the years, I've made variations of that dish many times over.

MAKES 4 SERVINGS

3 tablespoons extra-virgin olive oil

6 garlic cloves, smashed

2 teaspoons Calabrian hot crushed chili

1 (28-ounce) can whole peeled tomatoes

2 teaspoons granulated white sugar

1 teaspoon kosher salt

1 pound medium shrimp, peeled and deveined, with tail on

½ cup brine-packed capers, drained

12 ounces linguine, cooked

Heat a large skillet over medium heat. Add the oil. Add the garlic and let it turn golden brown; this should happen in under a minute. Add the hot crushed chili and stir for 30 seconds, so the chili blooms in the oil. Then add the tomatoes, sugar, and salt. Mix well. Lower the heat and let the tomatoes break down and cook for 20 minutes. Turn the heat back to high, toss in the shrimp and capers, and cook, stirring occasionally for 3 to 4 minutes until the shrimp is cooked. Remove from the heat and serve over linguini.

NOTES

Find an Italian market, and you'll be able to source the Calabrian hot crushed chili. If you can't find it, use regular crushed chili flakes.

CHAPTER SIX:

poultry dishes
from near *and* far

Crucian Curry Chicken

"Come to the island," my dear friend Chef Digby Stridiron teased, smiling at me as if my acceptance of his generous invitation to join him in the US Virgin Islands were a foregone conclusion. "The food, the lush scenery, the gentle island breezes," he continued, "you'll fall in love, just like I have." I'm not quite sure why it took me so long to take him up on it, besides the ongoing obligations of running my business, writing a cookbook, filing my newspaper columns, doing my advocacy work, and raising a son. Eventually, I did get around to saying yes. I excitedly packed my bags and went to meet him in St. Croix. What awaited me were endless blue seas, the warmth of his home, and this saucy Crucian Curry Chicken, seasoned island-style with allspice, cumin, lime leaf, and coconut milk. Have some roti or flatbread on hand to scoop up all the scrumptious sauce.

MAKES 4 SERVINGS

8 boneless, skin-on chicken thighs (about 2 pounds)

1 teaspoon coarsely ground black pepper

2 teaspoons coarsely ground allspice

3 teaspoons kosher salt, divided

2 tablespoons coconut oil

1 tablespoon vegetable oil

2 medium red onions, thinly sliced

8 garlic cloves, finely chopped

½ habanero pepper, finely chopped

1 teaspoon coarsely ground cumin seeds

2 teaspoons curry powder

2 Makrut lime leaves

1 fresh or dry bay leaf

1 cup chicken broth

½ pound baby red bliss potatoes, cut in half

½ pound fresh or frozen pearl onions, cut in half

1 cup coconut milk

½ cup cilantro leaves

Season the chicken thighs with the black pepper, allspice, and 1 teaspoon of kosher salt. Heat a large pan on medium heat. Add the coconut oil and 1 tablespoon of the vegetable oil to the pan. Place the chicken thighs in the pan and brown on both sides for about 2 minutes on each side.

Remove the chicken from the pan and set aside. Add the red onions, garlic, and habanero to the pan. Cook for 2 minutes. Add the cumin seeds, curry powder, lime leaves, bay leaf, and 1 teaspoon of the salt; mix well and cook for another 2 minutes. Add the chicken broth and simmer for another 2 minutes. Add the chicken back to the pan and cook covered for 15 minutes. While the chicken is cooking, preheat the oven to 400°F, season the potatoes and pearl onions with 1 teaspoon of the kosher salt, and drizzle 1 tablespoon of the coconut oil, and mix well. Put the potatoes and pearl onions on a sheet pan and place in the oven for 15 minutes. Remove from the oven and add the potatoes and onions to the curry chicken. Add the coconut milk and mix well.

Simmer for another 10 minutes. Remove from the heat and garnish with cilantro leaves. Serve immediately, right out of the pot.

Chicken and Mushrooms in Coconut Gravy

As Plato said, "Necessity is the mother of invention," and, as Disraeli said, "Variety is the mother of enjoyment." One fortuitous night, I was exhausted from a long day at work and was determined to figure out something to make for dinner without running to the market. All I had on hand were some chicken leg quarters, shiitakes, and dill in the refrigerator and my ever-present stash of coconut milk in the pantry. Well, "Voilà!" One of my new favorite dishes came together. To round out the meal, serve this homey dish with a green salad and a side of fresh fruit. Adding a glass of Gamay makes a beautiful end to a hectic day.

MAKES 4 SERVINGS

4 chicken legs

4 chicken thighs, bone in and skin on

4 teaspoons coarsely ground black pepper

2 teaspoons kosher salt

3 tablespoons olive oil

½ pound shiitake mushrooms

2 tablespoons unsalted butter

1 tablespoon unbleached all-purpose flour

2 cups coconut milk

½ cup chopped fresh dill

Pat the chicken legs and thighs dry. Season with the black pepper and salt. Heat a large skillet on high. Add the olive oil. Add the chicken legs and thighs, and sear well on all sides until there is a golden color on the chicken. Then lower the heat to medium and cook for 10 minutes, covered, until the chicken is cooked through. Remove the chicken and set aside.

Add the mushrooms to the pan and cook for 3 minutes, stirring occasionally. Remove the mushrooms and any drippings from the pan and set aside. Add the butter to the same pan, add the flour and make a roux. Add the coconut milk slowly to the roux and mix well until a nice gravy is formed; this should take about 5 minutes. Make sure you are stirring the gravy constantly. Add the chicken and mushrooms back to the gravy. Let it simmer for 5 minutes. Remove from the pan and garnish with fresh dill.

NOTES
If you ever wonder why different cans of coconut milk have different consistencies, you should know that there are three presses for coconut milk. The first press is the creamiest and thickest. Depending on the brand, you get different presses of coconut milk. My favorite brand is Chacko from Thailand.

Turmeric Lemon Chicken

Weeknight goodness alert! It's so easy to reach for boneless, skinless chicken breast halves when you need dinner in a snap. But, let's face it, they can be mighty boring. Well, not anymore! I got you covered. The staid, old standby, lemon pepper chicken, gains new appeal when it is punched up with turmeric, shallots, white wine, and bright parsley. You can even trot this crispy, coated delight out for a weekend date night when served with Jade Salad (page 39).

MAKES 4 SERVINGS

4 chicken breast cutlets

2 teaspoons kosher salt, divided

2 large eggs, beaten

1 cup fine dry breadcrumbs

¼ cup olive oil

2 small shallots, peeled and quartered

2 tablespoons finely chopped garlic

2 teaspoons turmeric powder

2 teaspoons coarsely ground black pepper

¼ cup dry white wine

2 tablespoons freshly squeezed lemon juice

1 tablespoon lemon zest

4 lemon slices

2 tablespoons pomegranate seeds

¼ cup chopped fresh parsley

Pat the cutlets dry and season with 1 teaspoon salt. Dip the cutlets in the beaten eggs. Then dredge them in the breadcrumbs and set aside. Heat a large skillet on medium heat, and add the oil. When the oil is hot add the breaded cutlets to the oil and fry them until they turn golden brown, turning once. This should take about 3 minutes on each side. Remove the cutlets from the pan and set aside.

Add to the pan the shallots, garlic, turmeric, and black pepper, and mix them well. Cook until the garlic is golden brown and the shallots are translucent; this should take less than a minute over medium heat. Add the wine, lemon juice, lemon zest, and 1 teaspoon of salt to the pan; bring the liquid to a simmer. Place the cutlets back in the pan and cook on a low heat for 8 to 10 minutes, until the chicken is cooked through. Do not flip the cutlets. Remove from the heat. Garnish with lemon slices, fresh pomegranate seeds and parsley. Serve immediately.

NOTES
The chicken does not have to be cooked through when you're getting it golden brown and removing it from the heat to make your lemon sauce. It will finish cooking in the lemon sauce.

Chicken and Andouille Sausage Perloo

I'm a Southern gal through and through, and this dish reflects my continuing love affair with dishes from the southeastern coast. I'm drawn to recipes that have a rich history, and when it comes to dishes from the South, that past can be fraught with pain at times, though so much beauty has come from that history. We gather around tables, pay tribute to tradition, and make meals that bring us joy. For me, this is the essence of the South.

Years ago, I was visiting Charleston, South Carolina, and my friend, Chef Kevin Mitchell, introduced me to Gullah cuisine. He invited me to a dinner where he cooked seven different types of Perloo, a dish similar to jambalaya. He had versions made with fish, crab, chicken, and sausage. It reminded me of the fact that every culture, no matter where in the world, has an iconic rice dish that highlights its cuisine. This dish is my homage to the people and place I adore: the coastal islands of Carolina and Georgia.

MAKES 8 SERVINGS

2 pounds boneless, skin-on chicken thighs (8 thighs)

2 tablespoons kosher salt

2 teaspoons coarsely ground black pepper

4 tablespoons olive oil

1 large Vidalia onion, thinly sliced

2 garlic cloves, finely chopped

3 fresh or dried bay leaves

3 sprigs fresh thyme

1 pound andouille sausage, cut into ½-inch circles

1 teaspoon sweet paprika

2 cups Carolina Gold or long-grain rice

4 cups chicken stock

2 tablespoons finely chopped fresh chives

Season the chicken with the salt and pepper, and set aside. Heat a large Dutch oven over medium heat and add the oil. Brown the chicken on both sides, then remove from the pot and set aside.

Add to the same pot the onions, garlic, bay leaves, and thyme, and cook until the onions are translucent, about 5 minutes. Add the sausage and paprika, and cook for about 2 to 3 minutes, browning the sausage on both sides. Add the rice, and place the chicken back in the pot. Add the stock and bring to a boil. As soon as the broth comes to a boil, turn the heat to the lowest possible setting. Cover and cook for 12 minutes. Turn off the heat, but keep the lid on for 10 minutes more. Garnish with fresh chives and serve.

Singapore Noodles

I've loved Singapore noodles ever since I first tried them at a take-out joint in Queens, New York, more than 25 years ago. I quickly learned how to make my own version and made it weekly during my college years. This dish continues to show up in my weeknight dinner rotation because Ethan loves it, too. And the leftovers are an excellent lunch for him to take to school. It also freezes really well, so I make extra. That way, Ethan can grab a lunch to go and zap it in the lunchroom. There's a lot of prep for this recipe, but it's super-simple to make.

MAKES 6 SERVINGS

1 (16-ounce) package rice sticks

2 quarts boiling water

6 tablespoons vegetable oil, divided

6 large eggs, beaten

1 medium red onion, thinly sliced

6 garlic cloves, thinly sliced

2 stalks Chinese celery, thinly sliced

1 pound boneless, skinless chicken thighs, cut into 1-inch strips

1 medium carrot, peeled and thinly sliced

1 red bell pepper, thinly sliced

2 scallions, thinly sliced

¼ cup low-sodium soy sauce

¼ cup rice wine vinegar

½ teaspoon kosher salt

½ teaspoon granulated white sugar

2 teaspoons turmeric powder

2 teaspoons crushed chili flakes

2 teaspoons garlic powder

2 teaspoons coriander powder

2 teaspoons cumin powder

Sriracha hot sauce, for serving

Place the rice sticks in a large bowl and pour the hot water over them, making sure the rice sticks are covered with the water. Let them soak for about 5 minutes; strain and set aside.

Heat a wok on high heat, add 3 tablespoons of oil to the wok and quickly scramble the eggs. Remove the eggs and set aside. Place the remaining oil in the wok, then add the onions, garlic, and Chinese celery to the wok, and stir well until the onions are translucent about 3 minutes. Add the chicken, carrots, bell peppers, and scallions, and cook, stirring occasionally for about 5 minutes, until the chicken is cooked through. In a small bowl, mix the soy sauce, rice wine vinegar, salt, and sugar with the spices. Add this mixture to the pan, and stir well. Add the noodles to the pan and stir-fry for another 3 minutes until everything is well incorporated. Add the cooked eggs and toss lightly. Remove from the heat and serve immediately with hot sauce.

NOTES

I like to cut the rice sticks with scissors into more manageable lengths when they are soaking in the water. You can make a vegetarian version of this dish using extra firm tofu instead of the chicken. Chinese celery is usually thinner, a lot leafier, and more potent in flavor than regular celery.

Pomegranate and Date Molasses Chicken in a Banana Leaf Packet

When I was still a restaurateur and owned my patisserie Spice to Table, this was an all-time favorite of our patrons. I created this dish so people wouldn't have to wait too long for something warm and comforting. These banana leaf–wrapped chicken and rice packets, tied with twine, would sit in a steamer, and people could order, pick up a package at the counter, run to the table and unwrap this subtly sweet, roasted chicken and fragrant jasmine rice parcel for a quick lunch.

MAKES 4 SERVINGS

4 leg quarters, skin on

1 teaspoon kosher salt

2 teaspoons coarsely ground black pepper

2 tablespoons pomegranate molasses, divided

2 tablespoons date molasses, divided

2 tablespoons honey, divided

4 tablespoons vegetable oil, divided

2 large yellow onions, thinly sliced

1 tablespoon soy sauce

4 sheets of banana leaves, cut into 12 by 12-inch pieces (see Notes)

4 cups cooked steamed jasmine rice

Preheat the oven to 375°F. Pat the chicken quarters dry with paper towels. In a small bowl, mix the salt, pepper, 1 tablespoon of the pomegranate molasses, 1 tablespoon of the date molasses, 1 tablespoon of the honey, and 1 tablespoon of vegetable oil to make a paste. Slather this on the chicken quarters, place the chicken on a sheet pan, cover with foil, and bake for 20 minutes or until the chicken is cooked through with an internal temperature of 165°F.

While that's happening, heat a medium skillet on high heat and add 3 tablespoons of vegetable oil. Add the onions, and cook them until they're golden brown, stirring often; this should take about 3 minutes. Lower the heat to medium-low, then add the soy sauce and the remaining 1 tablespoon each of the pomegranate and date molasses and the remaining 1 tablespoon of honey to the onions, and mix well. Cook for another 2 minutes stirring constantly, so the molasses doesn't burn. Remove from the heat and set aside.

Place the pliable banana leaves (see Notes) on a flat surface, and place a cup of rice in the center of each leaf. Divide the onions into four equal parts and place each of the onion parts over the rice in each banana leaf. Then place one leg quarter on top of the onions and wrap the leaf up, folding the two sides into the center and then folding the open two sides again into the center and tie with twine to secure. Place the banana leaf packages into a bamboo steamer with 2 cups of water at a rolling boil. Steam the packets for 10 minutes. Remove from the steamer and serve.

NOTES

To make banana leaves pliable, turn on a gas flame and run the banana leaves over the flame until you see the oils change the color of the leaves. This happens as soon as the leaf is over the flame. It should take no more than a minute to do all four leaves. If you don't have flame available, heat the banana leaf on a hot griddle until pliable about 5 seconds on each side. Make sure there are no tears in the leaves. If you find that the leaves are torn, double up on your banana leaves.

Turkey Moussaka

We visit our friends—Ethan calls them Uncle David and Uncle Martin—in Wilmington, Delaware, at least once a year. We share an extraordinary bond with them. Ethan served as the ring bearer at their wedding. It's a memory he cherishes. All this to say that our visit usually falls around the time of the big festival at the Greek Orthodox church up the block from their home. For years now, my favorite dish at the festival has been the moussaka made by the elders of the church. Well, since I can only have that once a year, I decided I needed to make moussaka at home, and here's my version of it with ground turkey. There's a little bit of prep for this dish, but the end result makes it all worthwhile.

2 pounds Italian eggplants, cut lengthwise into thick slices

2 teaspoons kosher salt, divided

5 tablespoons olive oil, divided

1 medium yellow onion, diced

4 garlic cloves, smashed

1½ pounds ground turkey

½ teaspoon cinnamon powder

½ teaspoon freshly grated nutmeg, divided

2 teaspoons coarsely ground black pepper

2 teaspoons sweet paprika

1 teaspoon granulated white sugar

2 teaspoons dried oregano

3 fresh or dried bay leaves

1 (14-ounce) can of crushed tomatoes

4 tablespoons sun-dried tomato paste

4 tablespoons salted butter

5 tablespoons unbleached all-purpose flour

2½ cups whole milk

⅔ cup grated Parmesan cheese

3 egg yolks

Slice the eggplants, season them with 1 teaspoon of kosher salt, place them in a colander, and set aside for 30 minutes to drain.

Preheat the oven to 450°F. Heat a medium Dutch oven over medium-high heat. Add 3 tablespoons of olive oil. Add the onions and cook for 3 minutes or until the onions are golden brown. Add the garlic and cook for another minute until it is lightly golden. Add the turkey and 1 teaspoon of kosher salt and brown the turkey meat with the cinnamon, ¼ teaspoon nutmeg, black pepper, sweet paprika, sugar, oregano, and bay leaves. This should take about 5 to 7 minutes. Add the crushed tomatoes and sun-dried tomato paste. Mix well. Lower the heat and cook for 20 minutes, stirring occasionally.

Line a sheet pan with parchment paper. Pat the eggplant slices dry with paper towels. Place the eggplant slices on the sheet pan. Brush 2 tablespoons of olive oil on the slices then put the pan in the oven. Bake for 15 minutes or until lightly golden brown. Remove from the oven and set aside.

Lower the oven temperature to 375°F.

Make the béchamel sauce by melting the butter on low heat. Whisk in the flour and mix well. Slowly whisk in the milk and cook for 3 minutes, stirring occasionally. Add the cheese and ¼ teaspoon nutmeg and mix well until the cheese is incorporated and you have a creamy béchamel sauce. Remove from the heat and whisk in the egg yolks.

Now it's time to assemble the moussaka. Lightly coat the bottom of a 9-inch cast-iron skillet with the meat sauce. Layer the eggplant and then the meat sauce, another layer of eggplant followed by the meat sauce, and then the eggplant again. Top with the béchamel sauce. Place the skillet in the oven and bake for 30 minutes until it is golden brown. Remove from the oven, and let it stand for 10 minutes before you serve.

Duck Confit with Pan-Seared Georgia Peaches, Caramelized Onion-Tomato Jam, and Cauliflower Puree

This is one of my favorite dishes to make for dinner parties. The duck confit, cauliflower puree, and the jam can all be prepared several days in advance. Once the guests arrive, all I have to do is sear the peaches. Since everyone gravitates to my kitchen, I'll pour some glasses of Burgundy and get a couple of guests to help with the plating.

If you don't have the time or inclination, purchase prepared duck confit.

MAKES 4 SERVINGS

For the Duck Confit

2 tablespoons salt, divided

2 tablespoons granulated white sugar, divided

2 teaspoons ground allspice, divided

4 duck leg quarters

4 cups duck fat

For the Caramelized Onion–Tomato Jam

¼ cup olive oil

2 large red onions, thinly sliced

2 large beefsteak tomatoes, peeled and thinly sliced

½ cup granulated white sugar

1 teaspoon ground allspice

1 teaspoon kosher salt

For the Cauliflower Puree

2 tablespoons salted butter

½ cauliflower, stemmed and cut into 1-inch pieces

4 tablespoons heavy cream

For the Pan-Seared Georgia Peaches

1 teaspoon duck fat

2 fresh peaches, peeled, pitted, and sliced into thick wedges

1 teaspoon light brown sugar

½ teaspoon kosher salt

To make the duck confit: Sprinkle 1 tablespoon of the salt, 1 tablespoon of the sugar, and 1 teaspoon of the allspice in the bottom of a container large enough to hold the duck pieces in a single layer. Arrange the duck pieces, skin-side up, over the salt, sugar, and allspice mixture. Sprinkle with the remaining salt, sugar, and allspice. Cover and refrigerate for 24 hours.

Preheat the oven to 225°F. Melt the duck fat in a small saucepan. Brush the salt and seasonings off the duck. Arrange the duck pieces in a single, snug layer in a 9 by 13-inch baking pan. Pour the melted fat over the duck (the duck pieces should be covered by fat) and place the baking pan in the oven. Cook for 2½ hours, or until the duck is tender and can be easily pulled from the bone. Remove the confit from the oven. Allow the duck to cool in the fat. Store the duck in the fat. The confit will keep in the refrigerator for several weeks.

To make the caramelized onion–tomato jam: Heat a medium saucepan over high heat, and add the oil. Add the onions and cook over medium heat for 5 minutes, or until the onions are golden brown. Add the tomatoes, sugar, allspice, and salt. Cook for 8 to 10 minutes, or until the tomatoes break down, all the juices evaporate, and a thick jam-like consistency is formed. Remove from the heat and let cool. This jam can be stored in the refrigerator for several days.

To make the cauliflower puree: Heat a 1-quart pot over medium heat, and add the butter. Once it melts, add the cauliflower and mix well. Lower the heat and cover. Cook for 8 minutes, or until the cauliflower is very tender. Add the cream and cook, uncovered, for another minute. Remove from the heat. Using an immersion blender, a regular blender, or a food processor, puree until the mixture is very smooth and creamy. This puree can be refrigerated for 2 to 3 days.

To make the pan-seared Georgia peaches: Heat a medium skillet over high heat. Add the duck fat. When the duck fat melts, add the peaches, sugar, and salt. Sear the peaches without stirring, until they are a golden brown, about 2 to 3 minutes on each side. Remove from the heat and set aside. Note: Sear these peaches just before plating this dish.

To assemble: If the duck, cauliflower puree, and jam have been refrigerated, bring them to room temperature. Warm the cauliflower puree in a saucepan over low heat. Remove the duck from the fat it was cooked in. Heat a large skillet over high heat. Sear the duck on each side until warmed through, then set it aside in a warm place. Prepare the peaches.

Schmear one-quarter of the cauliflower puree on each plate, place the seared duck confit on top of the puree, coat the duck with some of the jam, and lay the roasted peaches by the seared duck confit. Serve at once.

Quail Ragù with Piccante Frantumato

Some cities just tug at your heartstrings. Rome is one of those cities for me. I've been to Roma many times. Her history, her food, her markets, and her cobblestone streets make me fall in love over and over again. On one trip, Ethan and I rented a car and drove aimlessly throughout the countryside surrounding the city. We came upon a picturesque restaurant on a hilltop—Girarrosto del Buongustaio. When we entered, we were greeted by a gracious woman running the front of the house, whom everyone called *Nonna*, Italian for "grandmother." Her husband was in the kitchen cooking, and her sons were serving. I knew before I had eaten a morsel that we were going to have an incredible meal. I left awe-inspired. The ragù we were served that day has stayed with me. It just warmed our hearts and bellies. I remember speaking to Nonna and asking her what chili was used in the ragù, and she said *peperoncino piccante frantumato*. I found a market and brought home a bunch of that crushed chili pepper.

MAKES 4 SERVINGS

½ cup olive oil

10 garlic cloves, thinly sliced

1 (28-ounce) can peeled whole tomatoes

½ cup tomato paste

3 teaspoons *piccante frantumato* or crushed chili flakes

3 teaspoons kosher salt, divided

4 teaspoons granulated white sugar

8 whole quail

1 teaspoon coarsely ground black pepper

¼ cup finely chopped parsley leaves

12 ounces cooked orzo pasta, to serve

Heat a medium-sized Dutch oven over medium heat. Add 4 tablespoons of olive oil. Add the garlic and stir until the garlic is golden brown about 1 minute. Add the tomatoes, tomato paste, crushed chili flakes, 2 teaspoons of the kosher salt, sugar, and mix well. Lower the heat and let the tomato sauce cook for 20 minutes.

In the meantime, heat a large skillet with the remaining olive oil. Season the quail with 1 teaspoon of the kosher salt and the pepper. Sear the quail on all sides, getting them golden brown. Place the quail gently into the ragù and cook for another 20 to 25 minutes. Garnish with parsley. Serve over orzo.

NOTES

Frantumato *means "crushed" in Italian. The most common varieties in Italian cooking are Capsicum annum and Capsicum frutescens. Italian crushed red pepper has a rounded flavor with a heat that lingers, but doesn't scorch the tongue.*

CHAPTER SEVEN:

well-seasoned pork, goat, *and* lamb dishes

Lamb-Stuffed Eggplants

This recipe is an ode to Yottam Ottolenghi. Ever since I got his cookbook *Plenty: Vibrant Vegetable Recipes from London's Ottolenghi*, back in 2011, roasting eggplants and stuffing them has been a thing in my kitchen. I have stuffed eggplants with dried fruits, seeds and nuts, lamb, rice, and couscous; you name it and I've found a way to stuff it in an eggplant. I love a roasted eggplant even on its own, just sprinkled with some salt. It's the crisp skin—yes, I eat the skin, too—the velvety flesh, the charred, smoky flavor, and all of it makes me do a happy dance. I made a pilgrimage to London just to eat his food.

For the Eggplant

2 medium- to large-sized Italian eggplants, cut in half lengthwise, stem on

8 tablespoons olive oil

1 teaspoon kosher salt

1 teaspoon cumin powder

For the Stuffing

1 medium yellow onion, finely chopped

2 teaspoons coarsely crushed cumin seeds

1 pound ground lamb

3 teaspoons garlic powder

1 tablespoon mild harissa

1 tablespoon tomato paste

1½ teaspoons kosher salt

For the Garnish

1 tablespoon olive oil

¼ cup green or golden raisins

2 tablespoons pine nuts

2 teaspoons chopped fresh chives

To make the eggplant: Score the eggplants by cutting shallow cross-hatching across the flesh. Preheat the oven to 400°F. Using a pastry brush, apply 2 tablespoons of the olive oil to each half of the eggplant. Sprinkle the salt and cumin powder evenly on each one. Place the eggplant halves on a 8 by 8-inch baking pan, skin-side down, and place it in the oven. Roast for 20 minutes until the eggplant is golden brown. Remove from the oven.

To make the stuffing: While the eggplants are roasting, heat a medium skillet on medium to high heat. Add the onions and cumin seeds, and stir well for 3 minutes, until the onions are translucent. Add the lamb, garlic powder, harissa, tomato paste, and salt, and mix well. Lower the heat to medium and cook for 5 minutes, until the lamb is almost cooked through.

To make the garnish: In another small skillet on medium heat, add 1 tablespoon of olive oil, the raisins, pine nuts, and parsley flakes. Continuously stir for about 2 minutes, until the raisins and pine nuts are golden brown. Remove from the heat and set aside.

To assemble: Scoop some of the centers of the roasted eggplant halves, and push the roasted eggplant to the sides, near the skin. Don't remove any of it. Evenly stuff all the eggplants with the lamb mixture and put it back in the oven for another 10 minutes. Remove from the oven and garnish with the olive oil, raisins and pine nuts. Sprinkle the chives over the eggplants and serve warm.

NOTES

Scoring an eggplant is just like scoring fish or meat. Use a paring knife, make some cuts lengthwise from the stem down on the flesh without going too deep and cutting through the skin. Do the same thing horizontally at an angle as well. This allows the eggplant to roast evenly and have a more charred texture to it. It also looks beautiful.

Sometimes I serve these stuffed eggplants with a dollop of Greek yogurt or sour cream.

Pigs and Apples

Seriously, who doesn't love a pork chop? Here's a quick 20-minute meal for you. It's so simple, with minimal ingredients, that it almost doesn't seem right that it's so damn delicious. I've got nothing else to say about this recipe. Make it. Fall in love with it. Make it again.

MAKES 4 SERVINGS

½ cup unbleached all-purpose flour

3 teaspoons salt, divided

1 teaspoon crushed pepper flakes

4 bone-in (1- to 1½-inch thick) pork chops

4 tablespoons unsalted butter

4 garlic cloves, smashed

2 sprigs fresh rosemary

4 small Granny Smith apples, cored and cut into thick slices

1 tablespoon light brown sugar

On a plate, mix the flour, 2 teaspoons of salt, and pepper flakes. Pat the pork chops dry with paper towels, dredge them lightly with the flour on both sides, and set aside.

Heat a large skillet over medium heat. Add the butter, garlic, and rosemary sprigs. In 60 seconds, when the butter starts frothing, add the breaded pork chops. Let the chops cook on one side for 5 minutes until they're golden brown, then flip them over and cook for another 5 minutes on the other side. Using a meat thermometer, check the thickest part of the pork chop; it should be at 145°F. Remove the chops from pan and let them rest.

Add the apples to the pan and get them well coated with the butter. Add the remaining salt and brown sugar. Cook the apples on medium to high heat until golden brown; this should take about 5 minutes. I like the apples to still have a crunch on them. Remove the apples from the pan and serve alongside the pork chops.

NOTES

Support small local farmers. Don't shy away from paying a premium price for an animal that was raised and killed humanely. My pigs come from local cheese artisans who started raising pigs because they had all this leftover whey from making sheep and goat's milk cheeses. Their pigs are whey-fed, and the meat is far superior to store-bought chops.

Jamaican Jerk Pork Butt

I dated a dashing young Jamaican man for a spell. One of the things we had in common was our love of spice. He introduced me to authentic Jamaican eats. The relationship didn't last, but my passion for all things jerked did. Since then, I've vacationed several times on the island, exploring restaurants up in the mountains and along the beaches. When I feel the need for a little vacation vibe, I put some Marcia Griffiths and Jimmy Cliff on the speaker and slow-roast this allspice and pepper-flavored pork. I serve it with a big pot of stewed callaloo greens and pigeon peas with rice.

MAKES 6 SERVINGS

2 scallions, roughly chopped

1 habanero pepper

1 tablespoon whole allspice

6 garlic cloves

1-inch piece ginger

1 tablespoon whole black peppercorns

1 tablespoon fresh thyme leaves

1 tablespoon tamarind paste

4 teaspoons kosher salt

4 teaspoons granulated white sugar

½ cup vegetable oil

3-pound pork butt, cut into 6 pieces

Blend all the ingredients, except for the pork, in a food processor to make the jerk spice mixture. Rub the mixture on the pork and marinate in the refrigerator at least 8 hours or overnight.

Preheat the oven to 275°F, then place the marinated pork on a pan and place it in the oven. Slow-roast the pork for 2½ hours. Remove from the oven. Let it rest for a few minutes before slicing.

Pork Belly Sorpotel

The culture and cuisine of southern coastal India, from Goa to Kerala, was tremendously influenced by the Portuguese. They came as traders, following the spice route, and as missionaries, spreading Christianity. Christmastime is quite a big celebration in the region, and just about every Catholic home serves pork sorpotel during the season's big, family get-togethers. It is traditionally made with a combination of pork belly, pork fat, and pork offal, along with vinegar and spices.

In my version of sorpotel, I decided to use just pork belly and a ton of garlic. I think it's best to make this dish a day ahead of time, so all the flavors infuse beautifully into the pork belly as it sits in the rich gravy for a day. Right before you plan on serving it, reheat this dish over medium-low heat until heated through. My favorite way to serve this is on a potato slider bun to soak up all the fatty drippings.

20 garlic cloves, smashed

1-inch piece of fresh ginger, peeled and grated

2 small cinnamon sticks

8 cloves, coarsely ground

1 teaspoon cumin seeds

2 teaspoons coarsely ground black pepper

8 dried red chilies, soaked in ½ cup palm or apple cider vinegar for 15 minutes

6 tablespoons cane syrup

½ tablespoon tamarind concentrate

½ cup water or more, if needed

2 teaspoons kosher salt

3 pounds pork belly, cut into ¼-inch cubes

In a blender, combine all the ingredients except the pork belly to make a smooth paste or *masala*, as we Indians call it.

Heat a large skillet on high and add the pork belly. Let the fat render, and the meat get slightly golden brown. This should take about 8 to 10 minutes. Add the *masala* to the pork belly and rendered fat and mix well. Cover the pot with a lid, and cook for ½ hour until the pork is exceptionally tender. Remove from the heat and let cool. Place in the refrigerator overnight. Heat it up the next day and serve.

NOTES

It is essential to recognize that the fat rendered from the pork is an integral part of this dish. If you just can't help yourself and feel compelled to skim off some of the pork fat, do so after the dish is fully cooked. I strongly encourage you to leave well enough alone, though. The vermillion red fat is the most delicious part of this dish. It may seem like ¼-inch cubes are rather small. But that is what the dish calls for.

If you have a tough time finding tamarind paste, use tomato paste instead.

Garlic Black Pepper Pork

My mother, Hazel, often made a dish similar to this in India. The flavors were primarily soy sauce and garlic, as she didn't cook with fish sauce. Over the years, I have modified her recipe many times over. My favorite Cantonese take-out restaurant in Atlanta, BBQ Corner, makes something similar. I spoke to the chef, who gave me a few pointers on his version.

When I finally tried my hand at this dish, I loaded it with garlic and a heap of coarsely ground black pepper. One key ingredient is sweet black soy sauce. You can use dark soy sauce with a bit of brown sugar if you need to in a pinch.

Seriously, it is pretty dang good with just garlic, pepper, and soy sauce, the way my mom made it. So, if you find yourself short on ingredients, I permit you to make it a three-ingredient dish.

Enjoy this recipe, quilted together from visits to Hazel's kitchen, BBQ Corner's kitchen, and my kitchen. I hope it finds its way to your kitchen, too.

MAKES 6 SERVINGS

¼ cup vegetable oil

6 garlic cloves, finely chopped

1 tablespoon finely chopped fresh ginger

2 pounds pork butt, cut into 1-inch pieces

1 medium yellow onion, diced

½ cup diced red bell pepper

1 tablespoon coarsely ground black peppercorns

1 tablespoon fish sauce

1 tablespoon black sweet soy sauce

½ cup chicken stock

Steamed rice or broccoli, for serving

Heat a large pan or wok over medium-high heat, then add the oil. When the oil begins to shimmer slightly, add the garlic and ginger, stirring frequently until the garlic is golden brown, about 2 minutes. Add the pork. Stir well and regularly until the pork is almost cooked through, about 8 minutes. Add the onions, bell pepper, and ground pepper. Stir well and cook until the onions are translucent, about 5 minutes. Add the fish sauce, soy sauce, and stock, and stir frequently for 5 minutes, or until the sauce is slightly reduced and coats the pork. Serve over steamed rice or with steamed broccoli.

Dry-Fry Pork Mince with Green Beans

What can I tell you about this dish, other than the fact that I love Chinese food? In my college days at Queens College, Chinese takeout was a way of life. On the weekends, I'd find myself in Chinatown with my brothers, eating dim sum or finding a random little hole-in-the-wall joint that served the most delicious foods. My trips to any large city in the United States always have me looking for a Chinatown. My favorites so far are New York, Philly, Chicago, and a little Chinatown stretch in my hometown of Atlanta. I've been eating this soy-sauced dish of crunchy green beans and peppery pork for years in restaurants and at home.

MAKES 4 TO 6 SERVINGS

¼ cup vegetable oil

1 pound long beans, haricot verts, or green beans

4 garlic cloves, finely chopped

1 tablespoon finely chopped ginger

3 dried whole red chilies

1 pound minced pork

1 teaspoon kosher salt

2½ tablespoons dark soy sauce

1 tablespoon sweet soy sauce

1 tablespoon rice wine vinegar

1 teaspoon ground white pepper

2 cups steamed rice, for serving

Heat a wok over high heat and add the oil. Add the beans and continuously stir for about 3 minutes or until the beans are nicely blistered but still have a crunch to them. Remove the beans and set aside. Using a large spoon, remove and discard half the remaining oil in the pan. Add the garlic, ginger, and dry red chilies, and stir-fry for about 30 seconds. Add the pork, along with the salt, and continuously stir for about 5 to 7 minutes until the pork is cooked. Add the beans back to the pan and mix well.

Add the soy sauces, vinegar, and pepper. Stir continuously for another 2 minutes. Remove from the heat and serve over some steamed rice immediately.

NOTES

You can use common blue lake green beans or thin haricot verts in this soy-glazed, gingery dish. If you choose haricot verts, shorten your cooking time a bit.

Wild Boar and Poke Salat Lasagna

How did this recipe come about, you ask? Well, I was about to make wild boar and spinach lasagna and happened to call my friend and co-author Martha Hall Foose, who suggested I use poke salat instead of spinach. When she also sent me a link to Elvis Presley's rendition of the song "Poke Salad Annie," by Tonny Joe White, I was hooked! In the song they talk about a mythical-sounding plant that grows in the South and looks a little like a turnip green. I spoke to my local forager-farmer, and realized that it wasn't just a legend, and I got my hands on some poke salat. Of course, you may not have a local forager you can just dial up, so I want to assure you that spinach is still a great substitute for the poke salat—and mild Italian sausage totally works in place of the wild boar.

4 tablespoons olive oil

2 large shallots, finely chopped

8 garlic cloves, finely chopped

2 teaspoons crushed chili flakes

2 pounds ground wild boar sausage

2 teaspoons kosher salt

4 teaspoons light brown sugar

1 (28-ounce) can peeled, whole tomatoes

2 pounds poke salat, cleaned and chopped

16 ounces ricotta cheese

1 cup grated Pecorino Romano cheese

1 cup grated Parmesan cheese

3 egg yolks

1 (9-ounce) packet oven-ready lasagna pasta

½ cup shredded mozzarella cheese

½ cup chopped fresh parsley

Heat a Dutch oven over medium-high heat. Add the oil and the shallots, and cook for 3 minutes until the shallots are translucent. Add the garlic and crushed chili flakes. Mix well and let the garlic turn slightly golden brown, this will take about 1 minute. Add the wild boar, salt, and sugar; cook on high heat for 7 minutes, stirring often. Add the tomatoes and mix well. Cook over low heat for 30 minutes. Add the poke salat and cook for another 6 minutes or until the poke salat is wilted. Remove from the heat and set aside.

In a bowl mix the ricotta, Pecorino Romano, Parmesan, and egg yolks.

Preheat the oven to 375°F.

In a 9 by 13-inch pan, start with a spoonful or two of the meat sauce on the bottom. Layer the pasta sheets. Then add a generous layer of the meat sauce and spread it evenly over the pasta. Add another layer of pasta sheets. Spread a layer of the cheese mixture. Repeat this twice. On top of the last layer of pasta sheets, pour some meat sauce and then the shredded mozzarella evenly spread on top. Place the pan in the oven and bake for 30 minutes. Remove from the oven and let the lasagna rest for 20 minutes before cutting and serving. Garnish with chopped parsley.

NOTES

A cautionary note on poke salat: When poke salat matures, it develops purple colorations on its stalk and flower stem. Then it begins to bear berries and seeds. The MATURE leaves and purple stem and seeds contain poisonous substances. Young plants are safe to consume.

Goat Meatballs in Cashew and Roasted Red Pepper Curry

Meatballs, slow-cooked in a sauce, are universally acclaimed, from meatballs in marinara to stewed Moroccan meatball tagine, to Pennsylvania Dutch sweet and sour, to the hundreds of meatball curry variations across the globe. Every culture seems to have figured out a delicious way to cook them. Years ago, my Pakistani friend Sumaira's mom used to make this dish in their Forest Hills, New York, apartment, and I had the privilege of watching her make this dish on many occasions. It's essentially a goat kebab, stewed in creamy cashew and roasted pepper curry, minus the skewers. One of the flavors that makes this such a standout dish is *amchur*. It is sun-dried unripe, green mango, ground to a fine powder. Amchur imparts a citrusy sour note with a little bit of sweetness.

MAKES 4 SERVINGS

For the Meatballs

1 tablespoon vegetable oil

3 slices white bread, torn into pieces

2 tablespoons whole milk

1 medium red onion, finely chopped

2 tablespoons fresh grated ginger

1 cup chopped mint leaves

1 cup chopped cilantro leaves

3 Thai chilies, finely chopped

2 teaspoons cumin powder

1 teaspoon turmeric powder

2 teaspoons amchur (sun-dried green mango powder) or lime juice

½ teaspoon kosher salt

1 egg, beaten

1½ pounds ground goat

For the Curry

3 medium shallots, peeled and cut in half

3 red bell peppers, peeled, cut in half, and seeded (see Notes)

6 garlic cloves

5 tablespoons vegetable oil, divided

1 teaspoon kosher salt

1 cup raw cashews, divided

1 cup beef broth

For the finishing sauce:

1 teaspoon black mustard seeds

1 teaspoon fenugreek leaves

To make the meatballs: Preheat the oven to 400°F. Line a sheet pan with parchment paper and drizzle with oil. Soak the bread in the milk.

In a large bowl, use your hands to mix all the remaining meatball ingredients, except the goat, until they are well combined. Add the bread and milk mixture to the goat and mix well. Roll the goat mixture into 1-inch meatballs and place them on the lined sheet pan. Place the sheet pan in the oven for 15 minutes until the meatballs are browned. The meatballs do not have to be cooked through, as they will finish cooking in the curry. Remove from the oven and set aside.

To make the curry: Keep the oven on at 400°F. Line a sheet pan with parchment paper and place the shallots, peppers, and garlic on the pan. Drizzle with 2 tablespoons of oil and sprinkle with ½ teaspoon kosher salt. Place the sheet pan in the oven for 20 to 25 minutes until the vegetables are roasted to a golden brown. Remove from the oven and let the vegetables cool for 5 minutes. Place the roasted vegetables in a food processor, along with ½ cup of cashews, and pulse to make a thick paste.

In a Dutch oven over medium-high heat, add 2 tablespoons of oil. Then add the cashew-and-red pepper paste and stir well. Add the beef broth and mix well to make the curry. Let it cook for 3 minutes.

To assemble: Add the meatballs to the curry. Lower the heat and let the meatballs cook in the curry for 15 to 20 minutes until the meatballs are cooked through and the sauce is slightly thickened; remove from the heat.

To make the finishing sauce: In a small skillet over medium heat, add 1 tablespoon of oil. Add the mustard seeds, and after they pop, add the remainder of the cashews and cook, stirring until the cashews are golden brown about 2 minutes. Add the fenugreek leaves, mix well, and remove from the heat. Drizzle the tempered oil with mustard seeds, roasted cashews, and fenugreek leaves over the goat kebab curry. Serve warm.

NOTES

Ask your local butcher to grind your goat for you. If you have a tough time finding goat for this dish, lamb would be an equally delicious substitute.

I use a handheld vegetable peeler to remove as much of the skin from the red bell pepper as possible.

Kachi Goat Pilaf

I make this dish often, especially if I want something a bit out of the ordinary for unexpected guests. If I get a spur-of-the-moment night off, I'll round up some companions and whip up this pilaf in a pressure cooker. It's a delicious meal I can make in under an hour. Garnishing this dish with a mix of dried fruits and nuts adds crunch and color. The Mango Pineapple Raita (page 26) pairs beautifully with this pilaf.

1 tablespoon ghee or clarified unsalted butter, divided

4 teaspoons cumin seeds, divided

8 green cardamom pods, crushed open, with the seeds and husk

1 large red onion, thinly sliced

2 tablespoon garlic paste, divided

2 teaspoons ginger paste

1 cup plain whole-milk yogurt

1 teaspoon kosher salt

2 pounds boneless goat leg, cut into 1-inch pieces

6 cups beef broth, divided

1 teaspoon kosher salt

2 cups basmati rice

⅓ cup dried black currents

⅓ cup golden raisins

Heat the pressure cooker on medium-high heat. Add the ghee, cumin, and cardamom pods, and let the spices bloom in the ghee for a minute. Add the onions and cook, stirring for 5 minutes until the onions are golden brown. Add 1 tablespoon garlic paste and ginger paste, and stir for another minute. Add the yogurt, salt, goat, and 2 cups of beef broth and mix well. Put the pressure cooker lid on and let it cook for 20 minutes, about five whistles.

In the meantime, in a medium pot over medium heat, melt the ghee and add the cumin seeds and cook for 1 minute. Add 1 tablespoon garlic paste and 4 cups of the broth. Add the salt and bring to a boil over high heat. Stir in the rice and boil uncovered until two-thirds of the liquid is evaporated about 5 to 6 minutes. Set the rice aside.

At this point, your goat should be cooked. Open the pressure cooker and check that the goat is fork tender. If needed, reseal the pressure cooker and cook for 5 additional minutes.

Add the rice to the goat. Do not mix the rice in, just add the rice as a top layer, spreading evenly. Close the pressure cooker and cook for another 5 minutes, or one whistle. Remove from the heat. Do not open the lid of the pressure cooker for 10 minutes.

The residual steam will cook the rice through. Open the lid and spoon the goat pilaf onto a platter, fluff the rice, and make sure the goat is evenly distributed. Sprinkle with the currants and raisins. Serve immediately.

NOTES

Ask your butcher to debone the goat leg for you.

You could make this dish with beef rump roast or leg of lamb as well.

Leg of Lamb with Za'atar and Dried Apricots

Moroccan food really excites my palate. I love the kebabs, rice dishes, and slow-braised tagine dishes that are such an integral part of the food of this region.

Years ago, I had the distinct pleasure of having the renowned cookbook author Paula Wolfert in my kitchen for dinner. We talked about some of the similar seasonings used in each of our styles of cooking, like cumin, cloves, and cinnamon. I was so inspired by that evening; I remember wanting to cook Moroccan food for weeks afterward.

Another similarity between Indian and Moroccan cooking is the use of dried fruits in savory dishes. When fruit is dried, it intensifies the flavor and sweetness of the fruit, so when you stew dried fruits, it's as if the fruit blooms again as it cooks in the sauce. This dish can also be made with dates or dried figs and is absolutely delicious.

MAKES 8 TO 10 SERVINGS

2 large yellow onions, cut in wide rings

10 garlic cloves, smashed

1 cup whole dried apricots

½ cup olive oil, divided

2 teaspoons kosher salt

1 (5- to 6-pound) bone-in leg of lamb

½ cup za'atar (see Notes)

Preheat the oven to 300°F. Place the onions, garlic, and apricots in a large roasting pan

Drizzle ¼ cup of the oil over the onions, garlic, and apricots, then sprinkle with salt, mix well, Place the leg of lamb over the onions, garlic, and apricots. Coat the lamb with the remainder of the oil and evenly slather the za'atar all over the lamb. Cover the pan with foil and place it in the oven. Roast for 3½ hours. Midway through the roasting process, pull the lamb out of the oven and baste the lamb with the liquid in the pan. When it's done cooking, the lamb should be so tender that it falls off the bone and can be shredded with a fork. You can place the lamb on a platter, as is, or I like to shred the lamb and mix it well with the onions, garlic, and apricots and serve the shredded lamb on a platter.

NOTES

Za'atar is a blend of savory dried herbs, including oregano, marjoram, thyme, sesame seeds, cumin, coriander, salt, and sumac. Sumac gives it the citrus-like tanginess that genuinely makes this a "wonder spice" blend for me.

Finish off this dish with a drizzle of date syrup to add richness and intensify the sweetness of the dried fruit, if desired.

CHAPTER EIGHT:

beef *and* venison dishes *from* around *the* world

Braised Sambal Oelek Short Ribs

By now, most of you have heard about the chili sauce called *sambal oelek*. It is typically made from a variety of peppers with secondary ingredients like lime juice, garlic, ginger, shallots, palm sugar, and sometimes shrimp paste. It's a condiment widely used in Singapore, Malaysia, Indonesia, and beyond. It's a staple in my kitchen today, just like ketchup and mustard. This recipe calls for slow cooking. I could tell you to use an Instant Pot, but then your home wouldn't smell divine all day.

MAKES 4 SERVINGS

3 pounds short ribs (about 3 to 4 short ribs a pound)

½ cup of unbleached all-purpose flour

4 tablespoons vegetable oil

4 shallots, peeled and cut in half lengthwise

6 garlic cloves, smashed

1 stalk lemongrass, cut into 1-inch pieces

4 Makrut lime leaves

½ cup sambal oelek

½ cup liquid palm sugar or light brown sugar

2 tablespoons tomato paste

2 teaspoons kosher salt

Juice of 3 key limes

2 cups beef stock

Preheat the oven to 350°F. Pat the short ribs dry with paper towels. Put the flour on a plate and dredge the short ribs slightly on every side. Heat a large Dutch oven over high heat. Add the oil. Place the short ribs in the Dutch oven and sear all sides. Remove the short ribs from the Dutch oven and set aside. Add the shallots to the Dutch oven and cook them until they are golden brown; this should take about 2 minutes. Add the garlic and brown for 30 seconds. Add to the pot the lemongrass, lime leaves, sambal oelek, palm sugar, tomato paste, salt, key lime juice, and stock, and mix well. Cook over medium heat for 5 minutes. Add the short ribs back to the Dutch oven and mix well. Cover and place in the oven at 350°F for about 2½ hours. Remove from the oven and serve warm.

NOTE

My favorite brand of Sambal Oelek is Huy Fong.

Venison, Sage, and Turnip Shepherd's Pie

Deer season in Georgia runs from September through January. I'm lucky to have several friends who offer up some of their bounty. The deer spend the fall feasting on acorns, wild persimmons, mushrooms, grasses, and soybeans. The lean meat tastes of their environment. This potato-and-turnip-topped casserole exudes the autumnal taste of sage. Lima beans, carrots, celery, and corn stew in the savory gravy and make for a warm dinner.

For the Topping

¾ pound russet potatoes, peeled and diced

¾ pound turnips, peeled and diced

¼ cup half-and-half

2 tablespoons unsalted butter

¾ teaspoon kosher salt

¼ teaspoon coarsely ground black pepper

1 teaspoon finely chopped fresh sage

2 egg yolks

For the Venison Filling

2 tablespoons vegetable oil

½ cup chopped red onion

½ cup chopped celery

2 carrots, peeled and finely chopped

2 tablespoons finely chopped garlic

1¼ pounds ground venison

1 teaspoon kosher salt

½ teaspoon freshly ground black pepper

1 tablespoon Worcestershire sauce

2 tablespoons unbleached all-purpose flour

1 tablespoon sun-dried tomato paste

1 cup beef stock

1 teaspoon chopped fresh sage leaves

½ cup fresh or frozen (thawed) corn kernels

½ cup frozen (thawed) or blanched fresh lima beans

To make the topping: In a medium pot, cover the potatoes and turnips by at least 2 inches of water. Bring to a boil over high heat. Reduce the heat to medium and boil for 15 to 20 minutes or until very soft. Start preparing the venison filling.

Drain the potatoes and turnips thoroughly, and return them to the pot. Mash the potatoes and turnips. Add the half-and-half, butter, salt, and pepper, and continue to mash until smooth. Stir in the sage and egg yolks, and set aside.

To make the venison filling: Preheat the oven to 400°F. Butter a 2-quart casserole dish. Heat a large skillet over medium-high heat. Add the oil. Add the onion, celery, and carrots. Cook, stirring occasionally for 5 to

6 minutes, or until the vegetables are slightly tender and beginning to brown. Add the garlic, venison, salt, pepper, and Worcestershire sauce. Cook until browned, about 5 minutes. Sprinkle the flour over the meat mixture and cook, stirring for 1 minute. Add the tomato paste, stock, and sage; stir to combine. Increase the heat to high and bring to a boil. Reduce the heat to medium-low and simmer for 10 to 12 minutes or until gravy-like. Stir in the corn and lima beans. Pour into the prepared casserole dish.

To assemble: Spread the mashed potato–and–turnip mixture over the filling, making sure to spread all the way to the edges of the dish. Bake for 25 minutes or until the topping is browned. Allow to cool for 10 minutes before serving.

Spice-Rubbed Rib-Eye Steaks

Usually, I'm an eyeballer and poker when I'm cooking, trusting myself to know when things are done. But, when I've ponied up the big bucks for an excellent steak, I rely on a meat thermometer to alert me when the steak has reached the optimum temperature. I've become a fan of the reverse-sear method for cooking steaks. Starting them in a low oven until they just reach rare and then flash-searing them in a blistering-hot pan. Then I let nutty, cultured butter melt over the charred, crispy surface and pool up in the nooks.

For the Spice Rub

1 tablespoon black peppercorns

1 tablespoon flaky sea salt

1 tablespoon coriander seeds

1 tablespoon dill seeds

½ teaspoon granulated garlic

½ teaspoon onion powder

¼ teaspoon ground allspice

For the Steaks

4 (16- to 18-ounce) bone-in rib-eye steaks

½ stick (4 tablespoons) cold, cultured, salted butter, cut into 1 tablespoon pats

1 head of garlic, cut in half widthwise

To make the spice rub: Crush all of the ingredients with a mortar and pestle or pulse in a spice grinder.

To make the steaks: Line a sheet pan with parchment paper and set a baking rack over the paper. Remove the steaks from the refrigerator. Pat dry with paper towels. Scrape the surface of each steak with the tines of a fork, making sure to score any fatty edges. Rub each steak all over with the spice rub and place on the rack. Let the steaks sit uncovered for 1 hour.

Heat the oven to 225°F. Place the sheet pan with the steaks on the rack in the oven. Roast the steaks until they have an internal temperature of 115°F. This will take about 20 to 25 minutes.

Remove the sheet pan from the oven.

Heat a large cast-iron skillet over high heat until it is ripping hot. Add the butter and the garlic to the pan. Working one at a time, sear each steak on all sides, using tongs to hold the steaks down when it is time to sear the edges. Return each steak to the rack and tent with foil while cooking the remaining steaks. An internal temperature of 130° F will yield a medium rare steak.

Serve the steaks with a pat of cultured butter on top.

NOTES

I like to use a bacon press or a slightly smaller cast-iron skillet to weigh down the steak as the flat sides sears to ensure that the steak is making good contact with the hot skillet.

I also like to use a probe thermometer that sounds when the meat is ready; that way, as the steaks are cooking I can make a big salad to serve alongside these buttery steaks. Jade Salad (page 39) is an excellent choice. If I'm serving these steaks with Gorgonzola Three-Potato Gratin (page 77), I opt for romaine leaves dressed with the vinaigrette used in the Nice Salmon Salad (page 36).

Braised Corned Beef Brisket with Grainy Mustard and Dried Figs

Corned beef brisket makes its yearly appearance each March for St. Patrick's Day. But I think it deserves more than one day in the spotlight. A lazy Sunday would be perfect, for example. Then you have a lip-licking delicious dinner and tender corned beef for sandwiches during the upcoming week. The sweetness of the figs balances the saltiness of the corned beef, and a swipe of grainy mustard provides a bite of heat. Pick up some rye bread for the sandwiches while you're at the store.

MAKES 4 TO 6 SERVINGS

4 tablespoons olive oil

3 large white onions, thinly sliced

3 garlic cloves, smashed

3 large carrots, peeled and cut into ½-inch circles

3 stalks of celery, thinly sliced

10 sprigs fresh thyme

1 (16-ounce) can whole tomatoes

4 teaspoons kosher salt

3 cups water

1 (3-pound) corned beef brisket, flat cut and rinsed

½ pound red bliss potatoes, cut into 1-inch pieces

1 ear of corn, cut into 1-inch rounds

12 dried figs, halved lengthwise

¼ cup grainy mustard

Heat a large Dutch oven over medium to high heat. Add the olive oil. Add the onions, garlic, carrots, celery, and thyme sprigs. Cook until the onions are translucent and beginning to brown, about 5 minutes. Add the tomatoes and salt, and mix well. Add the water, and let the liquid come to a slow simmer. Place the brisket in the center of the pot. Lower the heat and cook, covered, for 1½ hours. Add the potatoes, corn, and dried figs. Cook for another 20 minutes with the lid on until the potatoes are fork-tender. Remove the cover and cook on high heat for 5 minutes. Remove from the heat.

Transfer the vegetables and broth into a deep serving platter. Slice the corned beef brisket and place over the vegetables. Slather the grainy mustard over the corned beef brisket slices.

NOTES

Corned beef brisket is generally sold packed in brine with a seasoning packet. Throw all that out! There are two cuts produced from a whole brisket—"the flat" and "the point." The flat is leaner than the point and slices nicely. It is basically rectangular in shape, while the point cut has, well, a pointed end and is a little more problematic to cut. I prefer to use the rectangular "flat."

Caramelized Onion Beef Liver Alongside Besties Braised Red Cabbage

I was never a fan of liver growing up. I don't know when things turned around for me. I've heard Southern old-timers say your tastes change every seven years, and that might account for it.

Now, don't scrunch up your nose at the idea of eating liver or chalk it up to something only served as an early-bird special. These seared liver steaks have a sophisticated mineral flavor, and I like to serve them with sweet and sour braised cabbage, a specialty of one of my best friends, Ellen Barnard.

Now, set those assumptions aside and give this quick and economical dish a try.

For the Liver

1½ pounds beef liver, cut into 4 thin steaks

⅓ cup all-purpose flour, plus 1 tablespoon, divided

1 teaspoon coarsely ground black pepper

1 teaspoon kosher salt

4 tablespoons olive oil

1 large yellow onion, thinly sliced

4 garlic cloves, thinly sliced

2 tablespoons unsalted butter

¼ cup whole milk

For the Braised Red Cabbage

¼ cup water

1 teaspoon kosher salt

1 teaspoon coarsely ground black pepper

¼ cup red wine vinegar

1 tablespoon balsamic vinegar

¼ cup packed light brown sugar

2 fresh or dry bay leaves

1 teaspoon ground allspice

1 small red cabbage cut into 4 quarters, leaving the core attached

To make the liver: Season the liver steaks with pepper and salt on both sides. Dust all over with ⅓ cup of flour. Heat a large cast-iron skillet on high and add the oil. Place the liver steaks in the skillet and brown them on each side for 3 minutes or until lightly seared. Remove the liver from the pan and set it aside. Add the onions to the pan and cook for 3 minutes or until translucent. Add the garlic; mix well and cook for another 3 minutes, stirring occasionally until the onions and garlic are golden brown. Add the butter and, when it is melted, sprinkle with 1 tablespoon flour and mix well. Stir in the milk, simmer for 5 minutes until the mixture reaches a gravy-like consistency. Lower the heat to medium-low, return the liver to the pan, and simmer for another 10 minutes.

To make the braised red cabbage: Preheat the oven to 350°F. Mix together all the ingredients, except the cabbage, in a small baking pan. Add the cabbage to the mixture. Cover the pan with foil and roast in the oven for 30 minutes. Remove the foil and roast for another 10 minutes.

To assemble: Serve the braised red cabbage alongside the warm beef liver.

NOTE

You can have your butcher slice the beef liver into steaks if you like.

Stewed Venison with Red Wine–Clove Reduction

꙳ ꙳

I grew up with avid hunters in the south of India. When we were young, my uncles and cousins would go hunting and bring back chital or axis deer, and a Siberian bird called koongh. The women of the house prepared a feast, much like what happens all around the world.

For a few years after college, I taught skin care and makeup at the Christine Valmy International School for Esthetics in New York City. My Venezuelan boss, Señor Bohorquez, was an avid hunter and would invite me to his home for dinner with his family after his hunting excursions. This dish is his recipe, which I enjoyed on many an occasion in his home. At our house, we serve this robust dish over potatoes roasted with rosemary. Venison stewing over a flame on a cold winter night is its own kind of magic.

MAKES 6 SERVINGS

3 pounds venison (from the leg), cut into 1-inch pieces

4 cups red wine (I like to use a dry Cabernet)

¼ cup olive oil

1 large yellow onion, cut into large chunks

4 garlic cloves, smashed

2 carrots, peeled and cut into 1-inch rounds

2 celery stalks, cut into large chunks

2 sprigs fresh rosemary

3 tablespoons kosher salt

1 tablespoon coarsely ground black pepper

2 teaspoons freshly ground cloves

2 cups tomato puree

Marinate the venison in the wine for at least 8 hours or overnight in the refrigerator. When you're ready to cook it, drain off the wine and reserve it. Dry the meat with paper towels.

Heat a large Dutch oven over high heat, then add the oil. When the oil is hot and just beginning to shimmer, add the venison and brown it on all sides about 6 minutes. Remove the meat from the pot and set it aside.

Add the onions, garlic, carrots, celery, and rosemary sprigs to the hot oil. Cook, stirring until the onions are translucent, about 3 to 5 minutes. Return the venison to the pot and add the salt, pepper, and cloves. Add the tomato puree and the reserved wine. Raise the heat to medium-high and cook until half the wine has evaporated. Lower the heat to a simmer and cover the pot. Cook for 2 hours, or until the venison is fork-tender.

CHAPTER NINE:

gorgeous desserts *and* sweets

Strawberry Chocolate Flake Pavlova

A floating cloud of sweetness! This crisp meringue, topped with succulent strawberries and luxurious Chantilly cream with a tease of bittersweet chocolate, is deceptively easy to make. Other than the cooling time, which ties up the oven for a spell, it really requires very little time to sling together. Slap-dash elegance works for me!

MAKES 6 SERVINGS

6 large egg whites

1½ cups super-fine sugar, plus 2 tablespoons for the filling and 1½ teaspoons for garnish

1 teaspoon distilled white vinegar

1 teaspoon vanilla extract

½ cup (about 1 ounce) very finely chopped or grated bittersweet chocolate, divided, plus extra for garnish

3 tablespoons top-quality strawberry jam

2 cups heavy whipping cream

1 teaspoon vanilla extract

1 pint fresh, hulled, sliced strawberries

Preheat the oven to 350°F and line a cookie sheet with parchment paper. Trace a 9-inch circle onto the paper (a 9-inch cake pan works well for this), then flip the paper over so the markings won't transfer onto the meringue. With a stand mixer, fitted with a whisk attachment or hand-held mixer, whip the egg whites at medium speed until foamy and beginning to turn opaque. With the mixer still running, sprinkle in 1½ cups of sugar in a slow, steady stream. Increase the speed to high and continue to whisk until the meringue is glossy, and, when the whisk is lifted, the peak slumps over ever so slightly. Add the vinegar and vanilla, and whisk for a few seconds. Sprinkle half the chopped chocolate over the meringue and gently fold to incorporate. Place a small dot of meringue in each corner between the cookie sheet and the parchment paper to hold the paper down while you spread the meringue.

Mound the meringue in the center of the traced circle. Using an offset spatula, shape the meringue into a round disk, smoothing the top and the sides while keeping it about ¼ inch smaller than the circle. Make vertical swipes with the flat side of the offset spatula all around the sides of the

meringue. Place the cookie sheet in the oven and reduce the heat to 300°F. Bake for 1 to 1¼ hours or until crisp and dry around the edges and the top. The center will be marshmallowy. Turn off the oven and leave the meringue in the oven until completely cooled.

When ready to serve, transfer the meringue to a serving plate. Carefully spread the jam over the meringue. Whip the cream with the 2 tablespoons of sugar and the vanilla extract until semi-stiff. (Be careful not to overwhip.) Fold in the remaining chocolate. Pile the whipped cream over the meringue and spread it a little shy of the edge.

Place the strawberries on top of the cream. Sprinkle with 1½ teaspoons of sugar. Sprinkle with grated chocolate.

NOTE

Just let your imagination run wild with variations of this airy dessert. Instead of chocolate flakes, perhaps fold in some citrus zest or finely toasted chopped nuts. Instead of strawberries, maybe use starfruit slices, orange segments, and orange marmalade, with a splash of Cointreau to ring in the New Year.

Triple Coconut Delight

It's a hot day. I have a craving for something sweet, but the last thing I want to do is cook or bake. So, what do I do? I pry open a few cans of coconut milk, stir the contents together let the concoction chill and serve over crushed ice like a New Orleans-style snowball. This icy dessert is popular in hot climes around the world.

MAKES 4 TO 6 SERVINGS

2 cups coconut milk

1 cup coconut water

1 (12-ounce) can young tender coconut, drained

1 (12-ounce) can toddy palm seeds in syrup

Pinch of kosher salt

4 to 6 cups of crushed ice

Combine all the ingredients except the crushed ice in a bowl and refrigerate for an hour. When ready to serve, place the crushed ice in small bowls and pour the coconut mixture over the ice.

NOTE

Toddy palm seeds, also known as Palmyra palm seeds are translucent with a jelly, candy-like texture. Leech fruit would be a great addition to or substitution for the seeds in this icy dessert.

With a little forethought, you can amp up the coconuttiness of this treat by making ice cubes out of coconut water and crushing them to make a base for the sweet topping.

Passion Fruit Key Lime Pie with Cardamom-Huckleberry Compote

On a trip to Savannah, I visited my gal-pal and a remarkable baker, Cheryl Day. She owns and operates Back in the Day Bakery with her charming husband, Griff. The place has become an iconic Savannah institution. I had the opportunity to spend a delightful, very early morning with Cheryl while she readied the shop to open for the day.

Before sunrise, Cheryl's assistants were rolling out, cutting, and baking hundreds of biscuits, and the scent of baguettes drifted through the air. Pies, cakes, and pastries were being created. The whole production was fascinating, and at the center of all this bustling activity was my ever-poised friend, who was clearly in control of the entire operation.

Cheryl baked me a key lime pie that day, and I shamelessly ate three slices in one sitting that morning. When I returned home, the memory of that pie stayed with me for days, I just could not get that pie out of my mind. My obsession finally drove me to pick up the phone and ask Cheryl for the recipe, which she generously provided. Bending to my taste for all things tropical, I made an addition of passion fruit, and for a colorful and flavorful contrast, I spoon a cardamom-huckleberry compote over each slice to add a little down-home flourish.

MAKES 8 SERVINGS

For the Graham Cracker Crust

MAKES ONE 9-INCH PIECRUST

2 cups graham cracker crumbs (16 crackers)

¼ cup packed light brown sugar

3 teaspoons cardamom powder

¼ teaspoon kosher salt

8 tablespoons (1 stick) unsalted butter, melted

For the Filling

1 (14-ounce) can sweetened condensed milk

1 cup heavy cream

½ teaspoon pure vanilla extract

5 egg yolks

½ teaspoon kosher salt

3 teaspoons cardamom powder

1 cup fresh key lime juice

1 teaspoon grated lime zest, plus more to decorate the pie

½ cup passion-fruit puree

To make the crust: Preheat the oven to 350°F. In a medium bowl, blend together the graham cracker crumbs, brown sugar, cardamom, and salt. Drizzle in the butter and mix with a fork until the crumbs are evenly moistened.

Press the mixture evenly over the bottom and about halfway up the sides of a 9-inch pie pan.

Bake for 6 to 8 minutes, until lightly golden. Let the piecrust cool completely before filling.

To make the pie: Position a rack in the middle of the oven and preheat the oven to 325°F. Place the prebaked pie shell on a baking sheet. In a large bowl, whisk together until smooth the condensed milk, heavy cream, vanilla, and egg yolks. Add in the salt, cardamom powder, lime juice, lime zest, and whisk until combined. The filling will already start to thicken at this point. Pour the filling into the crust. Bake for 20 to 25 minutes, until the filling is puffed up at the edges and the center no longer looks wet but still wobbles slightly; it will continue to set as it cools. The top of the pie should not be brown.

While the pie is cooling, in a small saucepan, over low heat, reduce the passion-fruit puree by half to make a thick syrup of honey-like consistency. Set aside to cool.

Cool the pie for about 1 hour until it no longer feels warm to the touch, then refrigerate until cold. Glaze the top of the pie with the passion fruit. Serve with the cardamom-huckleberry compote (see below).

Cardamom-Huckleberry Compote

MAKES ABOUT 1 CUP

1 cup fresh or frozen huckleberries or blueberries

2 tablespoons granulated white sugar

2 teaspoons cardamom powder

2 teaspoons cornstarch

Heat a small skillet pan over medium heat. Add the huckleberries, sugar, and cardamom powder, and cook for 8 minutes, stirring constantly. Add the cornstarch and stir well. Remove from the heat and let it cool. Set aside in the refrigerator.

Kirschwasser and Mace Double-Crust Cherry Pie

❦ ❦ ❦ ❦ ❦ ❦ ❦ ❦ ❦ ❦ ❦ ❦ ❦ ❦ ❦ ❦ ❦ ❦

Latticework makes for a beautiful piecrust. But I'm into pie as much for the crust as for the sweet fruity filling, so I like a full-on double crust. If the spirit moves you, weave a lattice top or Pinterest-up the top up as much as you like. You can gather the scraps to make additional decorations that can be glued in place with some of the egg wash.

Snack on a few of your cherries to see how sweet they are. You might want to add a squeeze of lemon if they are candy-sweet to balance things out.

Kirschwasser is a clear brandy, distilled from cherries and the name means "cherry water." The inclusion of the cherry pits, while it is fermenting, gives it a slightly bitter almond flavor. If you like, you can omit the Kirschwasser and use 1/8 teaspoon of almond extract together with 1/8 teaspoon of vanilla extract in its place.

Mace is a sister spice to nutmeg and comes from the brittle web that coats the fruit pit we know as nutmeg. It is usually found in pie spice blends, but is a true standout when paired with stone fruits and berries.

For the Crust

2 cups unbleached all-purpose flour

1 teaspoon fine sea salt

1 teaspoon granulated white sugar

1½ sticks (12 tablespoons) unsalted butter, chilled and cut into small pieces

¼ cup lard or vegetable shortening, chilled and pinched into small pieces

¼ cup ice water

For the Filling

5½ cups fresh or frozen pitted Bing cherries

1 tablespoon lemon juice

1 cup granulated white sugar

¼ teaspoon mace

3 tablespoons quick-cooking tapioca

¼ teaspoon fine sea salt

2 tablespoons Kirschwasser (cherry brandy)

1 tablespoon salted butter

For the Egg Wash

1 large egg

1 large egg yolk

1 tablespoon heavy cream

Pinch of fine salt

1 tablespoon decorating sugar crystals

To make the crust: In a large bowl, combine the flour, salt, and sugar. Add the butter and lard and toss to coat with flour. Using your fingers, work the butter and lard into the flour until the pieces are no bigger than the size of a pea. Sprinkle about ¼ cup of the ice water over the dough and mix with a fork to combine.

Form the dough into a ball and knead it briefly, folding the dough over itself. There should still be visible streaks of butter. Divide the dough in half and press each half into a disk. Wrap each disk and chill while preparing the filling.
Note: This dough may be made one day in advance and refrigerated, or frozen for a month or more.

To make the filling: Combine the cherries, lemon juice, sugar, mace, tapioca, salt, and Kirschwasser in a large bowl and gently toss until the cherries are well coated, and the tapioca is evenly distributed.

To make the pie: Roll one disk of dough into a thin 14-inch circle. Line a 9-inch tempered glass pie pan with the dough, letting the excess hang over the edge.

Pour the filling into the crust. Dot with salted butter and set aside.

Roll the remaining dough into a 14-inch circle. Place the dough over the filling. Gently press around the edges of the pie pan. Using kitchen shears, trim to within 1½ inches of the edge of the dish. Set the scraps aside. Fold the edge of the dough toward the center of the pie to make a rim. Using the tines of a fork or your fingers, crimp the edges to seal. With a sharp knife, cut slits in the top crust to allow steam to vent.

Make an egg wash by beating together the egg, yolk, cream and salt. Brush the top crust with a little egg wash (just until the top is lightly glossed). Sprinkle with decorative sugar. Refrigerate for 30 minutes.

Arrange the oven rack in the lower third of the oven. Heat the oven to 425°F. Place the pie in the preheated oven and bake for 15 minutes or until the crust is set and beginning to brown. Reduce the oven temperature to 375°F and continue to bake for 30 to 40 minutes or until the filling is burbling through the slits in the crust, and the crust is a deep golden brown. Remove the pie from the oven, set it on a cooling rack, and allow it to cool for at least 1 hour.

NOTE
Putting the pie in a hot oven will shock the crust and keep the from slipping down the edge of the pie pan.

Tres Leches Cinnamon Jasmine Rice Pudding

I do love a bowl of sweet, starchy, milky pudding, laced with cinnamon. I like to make my rice pudding with milk, evaporated milk, and sweetened condensed milk. It's a simple dish that makes a decadent dessert with humble ingredients. I enjoy this as a dessert in the evening and as breakfast on a crisp fall morning.

MAKES 4 SERVINGS

2 cups whole milk

2 cups evaporated milk

1 cup sweetened condensed milk

¼ teaspoon kosher salt

½ cup jasmine rice

1 vanilla bean

½ teaspoon confectioners' sugar

½ teaspoon cinnamon powder

In a medium saucepan over medium-high heat, bring the whole milk, evaporated milk, and condensed milk to a gentle boil. Add the salt and rice, and stir well. Reduce the heat to low and cook for 45 to 50 minutes, stirring often. Remove from the heat when the pudding is the consistency of thick yogurt. Scrape the vanilla bean seeds into the pudding. Mix the confectioners' sugar with the cinnamon powder and dust it over the rice pudding.

NOTES

This rice pudding holds up well in the refrigerator. You may need to stir in a little milk to loosen it up when it's been chilled.

If I'm having this pudding as a dessert I like it served cold, if I have a bowl for breakfast I like it served warm. I love it both ways.

Golden Carrot Halwa

For a short time in my childhood, we lived in Mumbai, when my dad's job took us there. The fondest memories I have of the city are my street-food experiences. The sweet shops were all lined with a colorful array of treats. This carrot halva was so very decadent. The texture is like velvet fudge on your palate. It was years before I realized how simple this dish is to make.

¼ cup ghee or clarified unsalted butter

4 cups grated carrots

½ cup whole milk

½ cup granulated white sugar

½ cup condensed milk

1 teaspoon cardamom powder

4 tablespoons almond slivers

Heat a nonstick pan over medium heat, add the ghee and carrots, and cook for 5 minutes, stirring often, until the carrots are very tender. Add the whole milk and sugar. Cook for another 5 minutes or until the milk has mostly evaporated. Add the condensed milk and cardamom powder. Cook for another 5 minutes, or until the halwa is thickened and all the liquid has evaporated. Scoop into small bowls and garnish with almond slivers. Serve warm.

Grandma Nisi's Rose Pound Cake with Saffron-Poached Quince

This cake is an homage to Ethan's grandmother. Grandma Nisi filled our lives with love, hugs, and a whole lot of cakes.

The scent of a flowery pound cake, baking in the oven, always reminds me of her. This cake, with its vanilla and rose essences, perfumes our entire home with an aroma that smells just the way love feels.

This basic recipe lends itself to all manner of toppings. Here I have included saffron-poached quince. This loaf is also fantastic with Cardamom-Huckleberry Compote (page 173) or the sauce for the Sticky Pandan and Date-Toffee Pudding (page 187).

For the Pound Cake

¼ teaspoon baking soda

1½ cups unbleached all-purpose flour

1 stick (8 tablespoons) unsalted butter, at room temperature

1½ cups granulated white sugar

½ cup sour cream

3 large eggs, at room temperature

½ teaspoon vanilla extract

1 teaspoon rose water

For the Saffron-Poached Quince

3 cups water

1½ cups granulated white sugar

1 teaspoon saffron strands

2 quince, peeled and cored

To make the cake: Preheat the oven to 350°F, and grease and flour an 8½ by 4½ by 2½-inch loaf pan. Sift the baking soda, and flour together on a piece of parchment or waxed paper and set aside.

In a large mixing bowl, cream the butter and sugar together with an electric mixer. This should take about 5 minutes to get light and fluffy. Add the sour cream and mix well. Add the eggs one at a time and mix for another 3 minutes. Add the dry ingredients to the wet mixture. Add the vanilla extract and the rose water and stir to combine. Pour the mixture into the greased and floured loaf pan. Bake for 40 minutes to 1 hour or until a toothpick inserted into the center of the cake comes out clean.

Let the cake cool in the pan for 10 minutes, then turn it out onto a wire rack. Continue to cool, then turn it right side up for serving.

To make the saffron-poached quince: Heat a 3-quart saucepan with 3 cups of water on high heat. Add the sugar and saffron strands and bring to a boil. Add quince to the liquid and cook for 30 to 35 minutes until the quince are tender. Remove the quince from the pot and set them aside to cool. Leave the pot with the syrup on the heat and reduce the liquid for another 10 minutes or until the liquid has become the consistency of a honey-like syrup. Slice the quince into ⅛-inch pieces.

Top the rose pound cake with the slices of quince and drizzle with the syrup.

NOTES

For the cake, you can use ⅛ teaspoon almond extract in place of the rose water to make a fine cake, but it will taste decidedly different.

Quince is something of the ugly duckling of fall fruits. It looks like a knobby pear and is tough as the dickens. But when quince is poached, it becomes royalty, developing a luscious texture. The addition of saffron to the poaching liquid here gilds the slender slices and brings their heady fragrance back to earthly realms.

You-Pick Blueberry Cake

One of Ethan's and my favorite activities in the summertime is visiting the many pick-your-own fruit farms on the outskirts of the city of Atlanta. A quick day trip is always a welcome getaway for us city dwellers. And we come home with pints of fresh-picked berries. When it's blueberry season, we make this cake many times over, and invite friends and neighbors for afternoon tea with this very cake as the centerpiece.

I'm not big on a sugary glaze, but I do love a schmear of clotted cream on this cake or a dollop of crème fraîche.

MAKES ONE 10-INCH BUNDT™ CAKE

2¾ cups flour, plus more for flouring the pan

1½ teaspoons baking powder

¼ teaspoon baking soda

¼ teaspoon salt

2 sticks (16 tablespoons) unsalted butter, plus more for greasing the pan

2 cups granulated white sugar

4 large eggs

1 teaspoon vanilla extract

1 cup sour cream

3 cups blueberries, tossed with 1 tablespoon flour

Clotted cream, for serving

Preheat the oven to 350°F. Grease and flour a Bundt pan or spray with baking spray with flour (I use Baker's Joy). Whisk together the flour, baking powder, baking soda, and salt in a bowl, and set aside. Using a stand mixer, fitted with the paddle attachment, or a handheld electric mixer, beat the butter and sugar for 3 minutes until light and fluffy. Add the eggs and beat for an additional 3 minutes. Add the vanilla extract and sour cream and beat for another minute. Start adding the flour mixture in, a little at a time, and beat for a total of 3 minutes. Using a wide flexible spatula, gently fold in the blueberries. Pour the batter into the Bundt pan and tap it on the counter twice to help the batter level out and prevent tunnels in the baked cake. Place in the oven and bake for 1 hour and 10 minutes. Remove from the oven and let the cake cool in the pan on a rack for 10 minutes. Invert the cake onto a serving plate. Slice and serve with clotted cream.

NOTES

Jars of shelf-stable clotted cream are available in many markets. Some carry it in the dairy case. You can also make an easy "mock clotted cream" by whipping 1 cup of heavy cream, then whisking in ½ cup sour cream or crème fraîche, ⅛ teaspoon of salt, and 1 teaspoon of powdered sugar.

Mango Cardamom Cake

From late April until early June, the most coveted of mangoes, the Alphonso, take center stage in markets across India. The luxuriously buttery, canary-yellow fruits are my favorite variety. I am entirely gaga over them.

This stunningly simple-to-make cake gets a lustrous, Alphonso mango glaze with the shortcut of using canned mango puree, making it a delight all year round. Festooned with fresh pomegranate seeds, the cake is a glory to behold.

For the Cake

3 sticks (24 tablespoons) unsalted butter, at room temperature, plus more for greasing the pan

3 cups sifted cake flour, plus more for flouring the pan

1½ teaspoons baking powder

1 tablespoon green cardamom powder

½ teaspoon kosher salt

1 teaspoon vanilla extract

6 large eggs

2½ cups granulated white sugar

⅔ cup canned Alphonso mango puree

For the simple syrup

1 cup sugar

1 cup water

1 teaspoon green cardamom powder

For the Mango Glaze and Garnish

3 cups canned Alphonso mango puree

1 cup fresh pomegranate seeds

A few pinches of cardamom powder

To make the cake: Preheat the oven to 350°F. Liberally butter and flour a 10-inch (12-cup) Bundt pan. Sift the flour, baking powder, cardamom, and salt into a large bowl. In a stand mixer, fitted with the paddle attachment, or a handheld electric mixer, cream the butter and sugar at medium speed until the mixture is light and fluffy, about 3 minutes. Add the vanilla and the eggs and mix until well combined. Decrease the mixer speed to low and add the flour mixture and the puree. Beat at medium speed for about 3 to 4 minutes, or until the batter is smooth. Pour the batter into the prepared pan. Bake until the cake is deep golden brown, about 45 to 50 minutes.

While the cake is baking make the simple syrup. Transfer the cake to a wire rack and cool completely in the pan. Invert the cake onto the wire rack, then put it on a cake plate or platter rounded side up. Poke a bunch of holes in the surface of the cake with a skewer and drizzle the cake with the syrup.

To make the simple syrup: In a small pot boil the sugar, water, and cardamom until the mixture is reduced to a thick syrup, about 8 minutes

To glaze and garnish the cake: Pour the puree over the cooled cake, then sprinkle with the pomegranate seeds and the cardamom powder.

Sticky Pandan and Date-Toffee Pudding Cake

I've always adored an ooey-gooey, sticky pudding cake. I've had some significant variations of this in my lifetime, but the best one I ever had was in Ireland. I found it at the local grocery chain in Dublin in the freezer aisle, and, boy, was it delicious. The next morning I returned to the grocery store and bought six of them to bring back stateside with me. I'm a sucker for a good sticky toffee pudding.

I've taken some liberties with this classic yuletide treat and whipped up my rendition with creamy coconut milk, dates, and pandan. Pandan leaves are commonly used for flavoring sweets in Southeast Asian cooking. The long spiky leaves add an aromatic, herbaceous note I find very appealing.

MAKES ONE 8-INCH CAKE

For the Date Puree

1 pound dried dates

2 teaspoon baking soda

4 cups water

For the Cake

Vegetable shortening, for greasing the pan

2 sticks (16 tablespoons) unsalted butter

2 cups packed dark brown sugar

3 large eggs

1 cup buttermilk

1 teaspoon almond extract

2 cups unbleached all-purpose flour, plus more for flouring the pan

1 teaspoon baking powder

¼ teaspoon kosher salt

For the Sauce

2 sticks (16 tablespoons) unsalted butter

4 cups packed dark brown sugar

2 cups full-fat coconut milk

2 pandan leaves, tied in knots

To make the date puree: Bring the dates, baking soda, and water to a boil over medium heat. Reduce the heat and simmer for 8 minutes. Remove from the heat and let the dates cool. Place the dates in a food processor and puree. Measure 1½ cups of the puree to use in the cake. (See Notes.)

To make the cake: Preheat the oven to 300°F. Grease and flour an 8-inch cake pan and set aside. With a stand mixer, fitted with the paddle attachment, cream the butter and sugar on medium speed for 3 minutes. Add the eggs one at a time, mixing well, then add the buttermilk and almond extract. Add the flour, baking powder, and salt, and mix for 3 minutes or until everything is well incorporated. Gently fold in 1½ cups of the date puree. Bake for 55 minutes or until a wooden skewer inserted in the center of the cake has moist crumbs attached, but no batter is evident. While the cake is baking, make the toffee sauce.

To make the sauce: Combine the butter, brown sugar, coconut milk, and pandan leaves in a medium saucepan, and bring to a boil over medium heat, stirring often. As soon as the sauce boils, remove from the heat. Keep the sauce warm.

To assemble: Remove the cake from the oven and let it cool for 5 minutes. Turn the cake out onto a serving platter. Poke several holes in the cake with a fork and slowly pour the coconut toffee sauce over the cake, letting it soak in. Serve warm.

NOTES

I like to make this toffee sauce even when I'm not making this dessert. I love drizzling this over vanilla ice cream or over simple poached pears or baked apples.

Any excess date puree can be used in chutneys or as a coating for roasted vegetables. I add it to Emerald Potion (page 11) or any morning smoothie or shake.

ACKNOWLEDGMENTS

With our first book, *My Two Souths*, my learning curve was immense and enriching with Martha Foose. This second time around, with Martha's steady and patient hand, it felt akin to enjoying the company of a treasured old friend.

We need fierce advocates—it is essential for business, for happiness, for life. Janis Donaud thank you for being my agent, without you none the of this would be possible.

A heartfelt thanks to Jennifer Kasius, my editor at Running Press, for believing that my culinary repertoire was more expansive than what I learned in my mother's kitchen in India. This book is a testament to that global vision.

Susan Van Horn thanks for listening to my vision and for creating a beautiful palette and framework to showcase the vibrant colors in this book.

Evan Sung thank you for once again capturing the essence of my food and bringing my story to life in vivid color! I am privileged to call you my friend and feel fortunate for this second opportunity to work together.

Clay Williams thank you for capturing the beautiful lifestyle shots in this book.

Thomas Driver I am thankful first and foremost for your friendship and your beautiful aesthetic that added so much to my food story.

Faye Poone thank you for being present through the entire photo shoot for the cookbook and making it a seamless process for me.

David Chang your unapologetic honesty about food culture has given me constant inspiration and removed so many mental barriers about a chef cooking beyond borders and not being defined by one regional ethnicity.

Michael Solomonov one life-changing meal at your restaurant and I have never looked at food the same way again. Solo, you may not know this but your food has been one of my greatest culinary inspirations.

Floyd Cardoz blazed a trail and kept the path illuminated for me and many other brown chefs, creating beautiful ripples of inspiration for many of us to follow.

Forever grateful to my brother Roy and sis-in-law Paula for their steadfast love.

Thank you with all my heart to Robyn Tedder and Ellen Barnard for being my "Sister Fires" in good times and bad.

Thank you George Crawford for motivating me to stay true to my authentic voice for this book. Your consistent encouragement to push me past the tough points and your enduring friendship made me cherish the experience even more.

Amma there is no me without you. I love you.

METRIC CONVERSIONS

The recipes in this book have not been tested with metric measurements, so some variations might occur. Remember that the weight of dry ingredients varies according to the volume or density factor: 1 cup of flour weighs far less than 1 cup of sugar, and 1 tablespoon doesn't necessarily hold 3 teaspoons.

GENERAL FORMULA FOR METRIC CONVERSION

Ounces to grams .... multiply ounces by 28.35

Grams to ounces .... multiply ounces by 0.035

Pounds to grams..................... multiply pounds by 453.5

Pounds to kilograms .... multiply pounds by 0.45

Cups to liters .... multiply cups by 0.24

Fahrenheit to Celsius .... subtract 32 from Fahrenheit temperature, multiply by 5, divide by 9

Celsius to Fahrenheit .... multiply Celsius temperature by 9, divide by 5, add 32

VOLUME (LIQUID) MEASUREMENTS

1 teaspoon = 1/6 fluid ounce = 5 milliliters

1 tablespoon = 1/2 fluid ounce = 15 milliliters

2 tablespoons = 1 fluid ounce = 30 milliliters

1/4 cup = 2 fluid ounces = 60 milliliters

1/3 cup = 2 2/3 fluid ounces = 79 milliliters

1/2 cup = 4 fluid ounces = 118 milliliters

1 cup or 1/2 pint = 8 fluid ounces = 250 milliliters

2 cups or 1 pint = 16 fluid ounces = 500 milliliters

4 cups or 1 quart = 32 fluid ounces = 1,000 milliliters

1 gallon = 4 liters

VOLUME (DRY) MEASUREMENTS

1/4 teaspoon = 1 milliliter

1/2 teaspoon = 2 milliliters

3/4 teaspoon = 4 milliliters

1 teaspoon = 5 milliliters

1 tablespoon = 15 milliliters

1/4 cup = 59 milliliters

1/3 cup = 79 milliliters

1/2 cup = 118 milliliters

2/3 cup = 158 milliliters

3/4 cup = 177 milliliters

1 cup = 225 milliliters

4 cups or 1 quart = 1 liter

1/2 gallon = 2 liters

1 gallon = 4 liters

WEIGHT (MASS) MEASUREMENTS

1 ounce = 30 grams

2 ounces = 55 grams

3 ounces = 85 grams

4 ounces = 1/4 pound = 125 grams

8 ounces = 1/2 pound = 240 grams

12 ounces = 3/4 pound = 375 grams

16 ounces = 1 pound = 454 grams

LINEAR MEASUREMENTS

1/2 in = 1 1/2 cm

1 inch = 2 1/2 cm

6 inches = 15 cm

8 inches = 20 cm

10 inches = 25 cm

12 inches = 30 cm

20 inches = 50 cm

OVEN TEMPERATURE EQUIVALENTS, FAHRENHEIT (F) AND CELSIUS (C)

100°F = 38°C

200°F = 95°C

250°F = 120°C

300°F = 150°C

350°F = 180°C

400°F = 205°C

450°F = 230°C

RECIPES BY CATEGORY

SLOW-COOKING SUPPERS

CELEBRATION CENTERPIECES

MORNING EYE OPENERS

SWEET GIFTS

AFTERNOON PICK-ME-UPS

HAPPY HOUR DRINKS AND SNACKS FOR EVERYONE

FRESH FROM THE MARKET BASKET

QUICK COOKS

EASY-DOES-IT DINING

FILLING FAMILY FAVORITES

GRAND FINALES

INDEX

Note: Page numbers in *italics* indicate photographs.